The Lean Recruiting Toolkit
An Agile Blueprint for Creating & Executing Top Hiring Strategies

CRAIG E BROWN

PREFACE

Welcome. I have intended this book to be a functional guide to creating and implementing efficient lean recruiting strategies at any company.

The first couple of chapters touch briefly on lean theory to set the stage. While understanding theory is important, the vast bulk of the book serves as a step-by-step practical process for the creation and execution of a recruiting framework, which will in turn enable you to find the best talent possible in the shortest amount of time.

I recommend you read it cover-to-cover in the order that it is written. Later, you can come back to individual chapters as a reference guide as and when required.

May I take this opportunity to wish you the best in your recruiting endeavors. Feel free to reach out to me if you have any comments or questions.

You are also welcome to connect with me on LinkedIn: https://www.linkedin.com/in/cebrownmba

Craig

ACKNOWLEDGMENTS

I think it only appropriate to begin by thanking my editor and dear friend, Holly O'Leary. Holly put in countless hours ensuring that this is a smooth read that makes sense; all in addition to working her own full-time job and raising a family.

I would also like to thank another talented friend, Ed Telling, for his work designing the cover of this book. A lot of people take good design for granted. I don't. Cheers Ed.

In addition, more kudos go out to friends Tim Brennan, Tom Dillon and Duncan Moss for being sounding boards throughout this process; Tim and Tom for their expertise in the recruiting field, and Duncan for invaluable tips on a writing a non-fiction work.

Also, I would like to give a big shout out to my friend and former colleague, Silvia Revenco, for teaching me how to source.

And last, but certainly not least, I would like to thank my family for providing the ongoing encouragement and support needed to complete this book. Thanks to my wife Anna, and kids Callum, Maya and Alex.

1. INTRODUCTION

When I was eight, I got a job as a paperboy. Willy, the boy showing me the ropes, assured me he had a good system in place. On my first day, he took me to the blue house at the beginning of Greenwood Avenue, put the paper inside the screen door, looked at me, and said 'see?'

I nodded.

Then, we then crossed the street to the opposite house, and repeated the paper drop. Open screen door, paper inside, close screen door. And then, strangely, we crossed back to the side of the road we had started on and dropped a paper inside the door of the house next to the one we began with. And then, you guessed it, we crossed back over again, and then again and then again.

As an eight year-old, I may not have been the sharpest knife in the drawer, but even I couldn't wrap my head around it. Why would you keep crossing the street? It was at least 40 yards, maybe 50.

'Why don't we just do the whole side of one street, and then come back the other?" I asked.

Willy shrugged his shoulders, and then carried on. He was retiring from the paper game and moving on to better things. His mind was elsewhere.

I have always hated inefficiencies. I know, 'hate' is a strong word. I loathe wasting my time doing one thing, when I could be doing something else more productive.

It's not that I am lazy - quite the opposite. Nowadays, out of all things on my daily 'to-do' list, I would simply prefer doing the things that result in a net-positive effect, rather than just putting out fires that could have been avoided. I actually have two columns on my list; one with a giant '+' above it, and the other with an 'X'. They all have to be done. I just try to minimize the number of things on the 'X' side. Anyway, back to my story.

The next week I had to tackle the paper route on my own. Here's the really weird thing. I didn't actually make any changes. I kept going across Greenwood Avenue, back and forth, back and forth (and the rest of the streets on my route), until all of the papers had been delivered. I had a guilty feeling that I could have done better, but in the end, I suppose I felt secure knowing that I had done precisely what I was shown to do. Who could get in trouble for that?

It wasn't until six months later that I decided to mix it up a bit - or rather, events forced my hand. It was a cold winter's day and the sun came up late. I was delivering all of the papers in the dark before school.

By this time, I was nine years old and hardened to the paper delivery game. And frankly, becoming somewhat discouraged with my job. It was boring, repetitive and now freezing, and I was aware, at least on a subconscious level, that I was doing more work than I needed to.

So, one cold February morning, I decided to do what I had wanted to do for six months. I started at the end of Greenwood, and delivered all the way to the end of one side of the street. I then crossed the road once, and worked my way back on the opposite side.

It seemed faster. It felt great.

I continued the rest of my route in the same manner - all the way to one end of the street, crossed, then all the way back.

When I got home, I looked at the clock. 8:25am. Something didn't seem right. I checked my watch and it said the same thing.

I got home 20 minutes early. It took me about 40 minutes to do a route that normally took 60. I was used to walking in the door at 8:45am, which gave me 15 minutes to get to school. Now I had loads of time to kill.

The only problem was I had this overriding sense of guilt. I was still earning the same amount of money, but not working as hard for it. It went against my blue-collar roots - work an hour, get paid for an hour. My dad actually asked me if I was delivering all of the papers. I'm not sure what he thought I was doing with the rest of them - bootlegging them in the school yard?

Anyway, the months rolled on and nobody complained. In fact, more people were getting their paper earlier, meaning they could take them to work, instead of waiting until they got home to read the funnies. I had unknowingly created more value by creating a more efficient system. Less time = increased value.

Lessons Learned

Lesson 1: Working more hours does not necessarily equate to getting more done.

Sure, for many manual labor jobs, you have to physically be moving to accomplish things, but for most intellectual roles this is not the case.

In fact, there is a pretty good argument to the contrary. Seven out of the ten most efficient economies (not to be confused with largest economies) in the world are in northern Europe[1], where employees take a lot of paid vacation days – the minimum by law in the European Union countries is a generous 20 per year. And, they are restricted to working 35 hours a week. They still get things done - more than most in fact. They are just hyper focussed when they are at work so they can then enjoy their time off.

Lesson 2: 'Inertia' is a hard habit to break.

People will keep doing things the same way because, quite frankly, it is easier. You don't have to learn anything new - you can just cruise on autopilot. It's also a fairly risk-free strategy for the individual employee. You've likely heard the expression 'Nobody ever got fired for buying IBM'. The idea is that choosing the safe option is the better choice professionally. If you choose IBM - and the project goes south, you can throw your hands up and say, 'Who knew?'

If you choose a lesser known supplier, and things go wrong, you'll be explaining your choice for quite some time. You might even lose your job.

---

[1] http://uk.businessinsider.com/the-best-economies-in-the-world-legatum-institute-2017-12

The problem is, while going the safer route may feel better for you professionally, it may not be in the best interest of your company. You have to be brave to break the inertia and make change happen.

Lesson 3: Change requires a catalyst.

In my paperboy example, the catalyst was that I was freezing my butt off and wanted to get out of the cold faster. Sure, I could take the easy route and say that it was the underlying frustration in wasting my time. But it wasn't. That was just not enough to get me to alter my behavior. It was the cold that tipped me over the edge.

So what does all of this have to do with recruiting?

Recruiting is, of course, much more complex than delivering newspapers. For starters, there are multiple stakeholders to consider such as the company, the recruiter, sometimes an agency, the Hiring Manager and let's not forget the candidate.

And there are multiple processes to take into account as well: consulting with the Hiring Manager, sourcing potential candidates, interviewing candidates, deciding on the hiring process itself, measuring success and so on.

And to make it all unbelievably complex, there are a few different ecosystems as well, each with their own behaviors and catalysts. There's the recruiting department, the company as a whole, the industry and then the overall economy in which this all sits.

But if we come right down to it - if we really get to the bottom of it - the same challenges occur in all industries and all departments, just with varying degrees of complexity.

With recruiting, as with delivering papers, working more does not equate with creating more value.

Tell me if this sounds familiar. You get a requisition to hire a new employee from a Hiring Manager. They want you to find a new iOS developer. You set up a time to meet with the Hiring Manager and quiz them on requirements. She tells you she needs someone very competent at the Swift programming language that has a rock-solid GitHub profile and multiple published iOS apps in the gaming space. You think it sounds challenging, but seems straightforward.

Once you have the information you need, you go away and advertise the role, and then start doing some serious searching. You begin to come across candidates who match the requirements, so you set up some screening calls. Over the coming week or so, you conduct five or six calls with candidates to see if they are as good as they seem on paper. Some are. Some aren't. You email the Hiring Manager with details of the best three candidates. Job done, right?

While you are waiting for feedback on your submissions, you strike up a conversation with one of your newer hires in the coffee room. You both chit chat about what you are working on. He is a young new Android app developer. When you mention your iOS role, he informs you that he might know someone who can do the job.

Long story short, this referral gets hired. And your searching was unnecessary. You could have spent your time working on something else, like onboarding, or annual performance reviews. Arghh!

The real reason you wasted your time is that you hadn't considered all the possible sourcing routes. It only takes a moment to think about these things, but if you overlook them, it can cost you hours of work, perhaps weeks of waiting.

And what about the point about inertia? We're all guilty of it.

It's very easy to just keep doing the same thing over and over. There is no risk. Or, at least, no immediate risk. We keep using the same hiring processes, the same software, and the same techniques when grilling Hiring Managers. We don't get the results we are hoping for, yet we keep pressing ahead because it is 'best practice'.

Yes, there is immediate risk in challenging the status quo. But there is also risk in doing nothing when the usual approach is not working. 'Hope' is not a strategy.

And the final point about catalysts? Catalysts have to be recognized and acted upon.

Within recruiting, catalysts come in a number of forms. In fact, some catalysts drop themselves right into your lap.

Picture this. You spend a week conducting some pretty intense search for a salesperson with all the skills and experiences that the Hiring Manager has requested. But the market is dry and you are stuck. The catalyst for change in this situation is the fact that you can't find what you are looking for.

So what do you do next?

You could try convincing the Hiring Manager that two years' experience will do, even though they asked for five. Or, you could consider hiring someone remotely who is capable of managing themselves. Or... the list goes on. The point is, you need to do something.

There are also times when catalysts don't get noticed unless you make an effort to find them. Try reviewing your recruiting plan once a week, just for a few minutes or so, to see how things are progressing. Try to actively find catalysts, and resolve them, so you don't end up wasting your time further down the line.

The key to both kinds of catalysts is to document your issues, decide on an alternative course of action, get sign off from the Hiring Manager, and carry on. We'll be discussing the two different kinds of catalysts in greater detail later in this book.

What's the big idea?

The whole idea behind this book is to provide you with a simple, yet effective, framework for creating a recruiting strategy for each type of role you recruit for. The strategy will consist of a basic plan, with the built-in capacity to revise it when new information comes to light.

It will save you time. It will save you money. It will save everyone a lot of aggravation.

What will I learn in this book?

This book is about change. It's about believing that 'good enough' is not good enough. And it's about having the personal drive to do something about it.

Here's what you will learn…

By the time you get to the end of this book, you will be able to create effective lean recruiting strategies for any role, resulting in faster searching and hiring, and better staff retention rates.

That's it. Simple right?

But if it were that simple, you would have done it already.

You can accomplish these tasks by following the steps in this book. Let's take a closer look at the main components.

Create a Lean Recruiting Canvas.

The Lean Recruiting Canvas is a one-page strategy document that encapsulates all the information you need to achieve fast, efficient and successful recruitment for one specific type of role. You'll have one canvas for your iOS roles, another for your Inside Sales Representative roles, and yet another for your Administrative Assistant roles, and so on. It will initially take you a bit of time to put your first one together, but after a few tries, it should take you no more than 20 minutes.

The Lean Recruiting Canvas will help you identify the business problems that have led the Hiring Manager to conclude that they needed to hire someone. We'll also look at Return-on-Investment (ROI) for new hires, in both financial and non-financial terms. And we will examine the recruitment Process, the Company's Unique Selling Points (USPs) and the Role Unique Value Proposition (UVP).

Then, once you have considered all relevant points and committed them to your Canvas, it will ensure that your plan is agile enough be adapted quickly and efficiently when you encounter a catalyst so you do not waste days or weeks looking for the wrong person. I've also built in a process to remind you to do quick periodic reviews to make sure you are on track.

Execute the plan.

It's now time to go out and start using the process you have learned. You will go through the hiring process you have designed.. Along the way you may encounter problems, or Catalysts. Perhaps there aren't enough qualified candidates in your immediate area. Maybe the Hiring Manager changed their mind on requirements.

The plan, or Canvas, will be agile in this sense: when new information comes to light, you will be able to quickly change and adapt it to minimize time wasting. You will also schedule regular reviews to see if any other Catalysts have crept in without being noticed.

Continuous Improvement.

Once the new employee is in place, you will need to evaluate how effective your plan was. You may not need to hire the same type of role again for a number of months. Having a record of what went right, and what went wrong can be very valuable the next time round and will save you even more time.

Who is this book for?

You will get the most out of this book if you have some basic experience in recruiting and placing candidates, enough so that you understand the fundamentals of recruiting.

You should also be ready, and willing, to make a change to your current processes. If you're not ready to implement real change, this book will be a waste of time for you. Go no further.

I had a few different types of readers in mind when writing this book…

Reader 1: The HR Director

As the HR Director at a large organization, you are fairly senior in your career and have been directly involved with most, if not all, aspects of HR over the years.

The other heads of departments at your company are concerned that your recruiters are unable to find the talent they require in a timely fashion. You know it's not because your team is incapable. Afterall, you hired them and trained them yourself. In fact, the recruiting agencies you have used have been equally unsuccessful in finding the required talent.

You have tried to convince the C-suite this is due to market conditions. Afterall, good talent is scarce in any economy - bull or bear. But, you are also concerned that when your team is actually able to find decent candidates, the Hiring Managers are too slow to respond and interview them. Afterall, good talent evaporates very quickly – great candidates will have multiple offers on the table. They don't need to wait!

Everything is happening too slowly for all parties involved. Everyone is frustrated.

Reader 2: The Corporate Recruiting Professional

As a Corporate Recruiting Professional, your job title may be something like Talent Acquisition Specialist if recruiting is your sole focus. If it's only part of what you do, your title may be HR Manager or HR Generalist. You have been in the HR field for at least a year or two. The HR Director is likely to be your boss, but if not, they will be two or three tiers up.

Recently, you have been getting both downward pressure from your manager, and lateral pressure from Hiring Managers. They both want you to find better talent faster.

Intuitively, you know that you can make some improvements to your own processes (and you may have been making already). You also know that your Hiring Managers could be making improvements. You need a solid methodology for convincing them to change their own ways.

Reader 3: The Start-up Founder

You have started your business in the last few years and things are going well. Sales are exceeding targets, and perhaps you have received Series A or B funding. The pressure is on from investors to build the team rapidly and scale up.

You were able to hire your founding team and first few employees from the pool of talent already in your network. That's great.

But somewhere between employee 5 and employee 15, your pool has run dry. You don't know any more people of sufficient caliber to work for your company and share in your dream. You need to hire more people quickly, but don't necessarily have the budget to hire a recruiter to work for you internally, or make use of local recruiting agencies.

You have made preliminary attempts to source new employees by posting job ads, but have been disappointed with either the volume or quality (or both) of candidates you have spoken to so far.

You have done some basic hiring before with other employers and need to expand your recruiting knowledge very quickly.

Reader 4: The Agency Recruiter

As an Agency Recruiter, you would like to increase your placement rate with clients. You have lost out on several placements in the last year because clients have been slow to provide you with feedback on candidates. The candidates - the good ones in any case - then move on to accept positions with companies that act faster.

Or the client either is not sure what they want, or they keep moving the target. Clients tell you they want one thing, then a week later, the requirements change. You get bored and/or frustrated and move on to another client.

You would ideally like a system that helps you minimize lost placements, and save time searching for candidates, by nailing clients down to both time frames and role requirements.

Regardless of what your background in recruiting is, think about the challenges you may be facing. Here are some of the more common ones:

- Candidates are waiting too long to go through the interview process
- Hiring Managers are not quite getting what they are looking for
- The company has ongoing challenges with employee retention

I'm sure you can add to this list!

Now think about actually doing something about it.

Imagine using a concise, slick, efficient solution that considers all relevant factors when creating your recruitment strategies that is also agile enough to allow for changes in direction triggered in an ever-changing recruitment landscape.

CRAIG E BROWN

What is Lean Recruiting?

The term 'Lean' has been bandied around the recruiting industry for a number of years now. The problem is that it just comes across as 'management speak,' without any real substance behind it - the flavor of the month, so to speak.

It sounds like someone took a good idea from another area of business and tried to make it 'fit' recruiting, like pounding a square peg into a round hole. I'd like to change this perception.

To begin with, let's have a brief look at the history of Lean as a concept. We'll then work our way forward to show how this applies to the recruiting field.

How did Lean come about?

'Lean' started with the Japanese manufacturing industry of the 1960s and 1970s, specifically with the Toyota Car Corporation, whereby a process was developed to make manufacturing more efficient called 'Just-in-Time Manufacturing'[2]. The very basic idea behind it was that manufacturers wanted parts delivered just in time to be

---

[2] https://en.wikipedia.org/wiki/Just-in-time_manufacturing

manufactured, rather than having large amounts of spare parts sitting on shelves gathering dust, waiting to be used.

There appear to have been a number of possible reasons for this.

'During Japan's post-World War II rebuilding of industry:

1. Japan's lack of cash made it difficult for industry to finance the big-batch, large inventory production methods common elsewhere.
2. Japan lacked space to build big factories loaded with inventory.
3. The Japanese islands were (and are) lacking in natural resources with which to build products.
4. Japan had high unemployment, which meant that labor efficiency methods were not an obvious pathway to industrial success. Thus the Japanese "leaned out" their processes.

They built smaller factories ... in which the only materials housed in the factory were those on which work was currently being done. In this way, inventory levels were kept low, investment in in-process inventories was at a minimum, and the investment in purchased natural resources was quickly turned around so that additional materials were purchased.'[3]

So, catalysts seemed to have been lack of space, money and natural resources. In short, Japanese manufacturing was left with only one option to be competitive; to overhaul the manufacturing process entirely, which is exactly what they did.

---

[3] https://en.wikipedia.org/wiki/Just-in-time_manufacturing

Fast forward a couple of decades and Just-in-Time Manufacturing was going strong. The terminology changed, however, to Lean Manufacturing around the early 1990s. The processes came to not only cover the timely ordering and supply of parts, but also began to encompass improvements in the entire manufacturing function. This is when we begin to see the term Lean referring to all the activities in a specific department of a business.

In the early 1990s, Motorola came up with, and adopted, a new process called 6 Sigma.

Like Lean Manufacturing, 6 Sigma also looks to improve processes, mainly in manufacturing, but takes a very statistical, highly empirical approach. Every single aspect of the process is measured so that it becomes easier to evaluate what is going wrong when something heads south.

While the term Lean works great for manufacturing, and to a certain extent other workflow-based processes, it has not really been used extensively with people-based processes. With people, there are ironically simply too many moving parts. We, as human beings, are arguably (and somewhat paradoxically) too complicated to measure.

The next relevant iteration of Lean came in the form of the Business Model Canvas, created by Alexander Osterwalder in 2008. This is really interesting work because it was the first version of Lean that attempted to encapsulate the entire workings of a company.

And, it was also the first version of Lean that used a canvas as a one-page strategy document. It was meant to help visualize all aspects of a business to aid in the identification of trouble areas and make a plan of action going forward. The boxes on Osterwalder's canvas include Key Partners, Key Activities, Key Resources, Value Propositions, Customer Relationships,

Channels, Customer Segments, Cost Structure and Revenue Streams.

The Business Model Canvas is a good tool for more mature companies as a high-level strategic tool but is not so functional for companies just getting started. They have different challenges.

And to the rescue comes the Lean Startup Canvas by Ash Maurya, which in turn was based on Lean Startup Methodology proposed by Eric Reis in 2008.

The Lean Startup Canvas was designed right from the start to be much more agile at dealing with new endeavors; namely start-ups. Start-ups often don't have a lot of money or heavy infrastructure (unlike manufacturing), so the idea was that once the business plan is mapped out on the canvas, rapid changes, or 'pivots' can be made when encountering resistance, changes or other unforeseen factors.

The Lean Startup Canvas consists of the following sections; Problem, Solution, Key Metrics, Unique Value Proposition, Unfair Advantage, Channels, Customer Segments, Cost Structure and Revenue Streams. Some of these sections are focused outward toward the market, and others are more inward focussed.

And now on to recruiting. The Lean Recruiting Canvas concept covered in this book draws on all of these ideas, but with changes to better serve the recruitment field. The recruitment function of a company is not a free-standing entity in its own right, but rather a department within a company, much like manufacturing in the first example.

The recruiting function is also light on expensive physical infrastructure and therefore an agile framework is most appropriate. Recruiting approaches need to turn on a dime, or pivot, when it needs to. There is also the duality of an inward and outward focus, much like start-ups.

We will get into much greater detail later about the Lean Recruiting Canvas[4], but I will leave you with the components to contemplate for now. These include Problem, Solution, Company USPs, Role UVP, Ideal Employee, Key Metrics, Process, Sources, Cost Structure and Value Added.

What's wrong with the status quo?

To an extent, I am preaching to the choir. If you are reading this book, you have likely already realized that something needs changing. Great start!

The recruiting status quo at your organization will currently fall into one of two scenarios.

Scenario 1: No current strategy

You likely find that you are quite successful at finding and hiring candidates a significant proportion of the time. The problem is that when you are successful, you don't know precisely why that is. And the problem with not knowing why you are successful is that when you become less successful, you won't know how to rectify the situation.

You could be strong in at several aspects of recruitment, but not as strong in others. For example, you may do well at Boolean search, writing job descriptions, and quick turnarounds, but are weaker in getting buy-in from Hiring Managers or measuring success. You have several important pieces of the puzzle, but not all of them.

---

[4] Available in the chapter entitled The Lean Recruiting Canvas.

You may very well lack a comprehensive plan of attack for executing your recruiting. If you haven't committed your plan to writing, you can easily get off track.

There is no mechanism in place for continuously improving the process. No Kaizen.

When you do make a mistake, or a Catalyst raises its head above the parapet, you need a system in place that will codify your attempts at improvement, so you can see where you have been in the past, where you are right now, and where you want to be in the future. Kaizen will help you eventually hit the bullseye.

The best example I can give you is from my own company about seven years ago.

At the time, I was placing mainly software developers, largely for one client. This company was a digital agency in Canada who mainly did outsourced work for a number of very high-profile clients in the US media industry.

Over the period of two of years, I placed more than 20 employees with them. The vast majority of these placements were Web Developers, iOS Developers and Android Developers. When I tried to replicate this degree of success with other clients, I was only able to do so sporadically.

I came to realize that my success with this particular client had not come from my efforts alone, but from theirs as well. They knew exactly what they wanted, and the candidates they wanted were the ones they actually needed. They never changed their mind and they had a very stringent, codified interviewing process they used once I handed over a candidate to them.

On occasion, they would screen someone out for what I might have felt was a niggly point, but in the end the results were good. Every placement I made survived their probationary period and stayed for a number of years, contributing great work along the way.

I eventually realized that to replicate the success I had had with this client, I had to become responsible for setting up, and managing, all components of the recruiting function, including getting buy-in from the individual Hiring Managers.

Scenario 2: Incumbent strategy already in place

The second possible scenario is that you already have a hiring strategy in place, but it really is just a linear process, maybe even depicted by a flow chart.

You've probably seen one before. It has a beginning, a middle and an end with a few escape loops built in to the process. On paper, it looks a bit like Chutes and Ladders. It starts with 'Receive Requisition' or something similar, and then moves on to things like 'Decide Selection Criteria,' 'Advertise Job' and so on. You get through a couple of interviews and then make the hire. The process was probably created by someone in the company a long time ago that no one remembers. It gets used because it's there and nothing else exists.

There are a few issues with this type of 'strategy.' The first is that it is just too vague to have any real meaning. It's a 'one-size-fits-all' strategy. It probably does, in theory, encompass everything you need to do to hire for a wide swathe of roles, from Administrative Assistants and Chief Financial Officers. But in an effort to be all-encompassing, it is missing out on the finer detail.

The flow chart approach means you either encompass everything and miss out on the detail, or you include the finer detail but cannot possibly include all types of roles effectively.

A flow chart is simply too vague.

By implication, flowcharts assume that individual HR Professionals have little value to add to the process. There, I said it.

Flowcharts are a top-down, ultra-prescriptive, micro-managed process. By being so prescriptive, it assumes that you are incapable of developing an intelligent, nuanced plan yourself. In doing so, it perpetuates the misconception that HR professionals don't really know that much about the business.

Time to change that misconception!

Rather than accepting a top-down flowchart, create your own recruiting strategies. After all, in the words of General George S Patton, "Never tell people how to do things. Tell them what to do and they will surprise you with their ingenuity."[5]

If recruiting professionals create their own strategies, these strategies can be granular, role-specific, and adaptable when faced with Catalysts. You will get to the finish line faster, and with better results. You can do it. You are, after all, an educated experienced professional.

The second real problem with flow charts is that there is no room for our Kaizen principle of continuous improvement. It basically assumes that if you follow the flow chart, things will work out every time. We all know they don't.

---

[5] https://www.wearethemighty.com/articles/general-george-patton-quotes

Certainly, if recruitment was conducted in a closed system, without being affected by other departments, the company as a whole, the industry and the greater economy, a flowchart might stand a chance.

But this is a pipe dream. You can't stop the world from spinning. And you can't stop external factors from affecting your recruitment efforts. What you can do, is adapt to them quickly and effectively.

CRAIG E BROWN

7 Reasons to Use the Lean Recruiting Canvas

Here's my short list of really good reasons to adopt the Lean Recruiting Canvas as your primary recruitment strategy.

1. The Lean Recruiting Canvas is a flexible strategy that fits all recruiting scenarios.

2. It is not just theory. It's a practical step-by-step strategy for implementing Lean practices.

3. It helps you get buy-in from Hiring Managers.

4. Importantly, it aligns business requirements with the recruiting function.

5. It increases retention rates.

6. It shortens your time-to-hire considerably.

7. And finally, the Lean Recruiting Canvas results in a more positive candidate experience.

Lean Theory 101

Before we delve into the more practical side of this book, namely the creation and execution of your Lean Recruiting Canvas, it is important to understand the theory behind your actions. That way, if you get sidelined, you'll have a good enough understanding of the theoretical context to help get you back on track. Think of this chapter as 'practical theory'.

There is enough material on Lean theory to write an entire book. In fact, many have[6]. I will, however, provide you with a high-level summary below, particularly as it pertains to the recruitment arena.

So, what is Lean?

When people hear the word Lean, quite simply they usually think about saving money. And when they think about saving money, they assume there is a related reduction in quality. This is not the case here.

---

[6] If you would like a bit of extra reading, check out *Lean Thinking* by Womack and Jones. Also, have a look at *The Machine That Changed The World*, by Womack, Jones & Loos, as well as *Lean Six Sigma For Service* by Michael L George. There are many more.

As it pertains to manufacturing, Lean 'is a systematic method for waste minimization within a manufacturing system without sacrificing productivity.'[7] Basically, it means cutting out all the unnecessary waste to save time and money, while maintaining quality.

This makes perfect sense when talking about manufacturing, when the principal characters are machines and associated processes.

When it comes to people-oriented systems, I would take this definition one step further. Remember this going forward, and even bookmark this page if you have to.

'Lean Recruiting' is a systematic method for waste minimization, while at the same time <u>increasing</u> productivity within the recruiting process.

Why the subtle difference? Machines can typically only perform one function or task. They have the same value per hour at all times to the company. If you minimize inefficiency, a machine will be able to produce more of that 'thing' it does or manufactures in a 24-hour period, providing more value to the company on a fairly linear basis.

People, on the other hand, are complex creatures. We can perform a multitude of tasks with varying degrees of value. If we reduce wasting our time performing one function of fairly low value, we can then spend that time performing tasks that produce greater productivity per unit of time. Value is then increased on an exponential basis, rather than a linear one.

---

[7] https://en.wikipedia.org/wiki/Lean_manufacturing

For example, if I trade ten hours of time performing Boolean search for candidates that are impossible to find, and trade that that ten hours for one hour of refining required candidate criteria with the Hiring Manager, plus two hours of Boolean search using the revised criteria to get to the right candidate, I am ahead of the game. I will be able to find a better candidate faster and save seven hours of valuable time.

Those seven hours can be then used to perform other HR-related, high value tasks, such as performance reviews, onboarding, planning Learning and Development programs and even recruiting for other roles on your desk.

Make sense? Good. Don't forget it. It's important.

What are the terms I will encounter?

Let's also have a quick look at some of the main terms you will encounter in this book so we are using a common vocabulary.

Lean Recruiting

As indicated above, Lean Recruiting is a systematic method for waste minimization, while at the same time increasing productivity.

In fact, we will try to get into the habit of only cutting waste from our recruiting processes if we are confident it will result in an exponential improvement in our productivity as recruiters. We will strive for perfection.

Agile

Agile means being able to maneuver quickly. More precisely, it refers to 'the ability to create and respond to change in order to succeed in an uncertain and turbulent environment.'[8]

It means that the plan we are going to make, the Lean Recruiting Canvas, is put together with the capacity for change already built in, ready to be shifted when Catalysts come to light.

Catalyst

A Catalyst, for our purposes, will refer to any event or circumstance that acts as an enabler for change to our plan, or Canvas. There are two types of catalysts: Obstructive Catalysts™ and Latent Catalysts™.

An Obstructive Catalyst is an event that takes place which prevents you from taking further action in your recruiting cycle unless change is made to the Canvas. It obstructs you from continuing down your current path unless you make a change.

For example, let's say you have searched for two weeks for an iOS Developer in your local area with the background and experience the Hiring Manager has requested. You have found no one. You are stuck. In order to move forward, a change has to be made to your process. If you don't make a change, no one gets hired.

A Latent Catalyst is a catalyst that only becomes apparent upon regular inspection. For example, you block off 30 minutes of your schedule every Friday to review your Canvases for the three roles you are working on to assess

---

[8] https://www.agilealliance.org/agile101/

your progress. You notice that the salary requirement for one of the candidates being interviewed is higher than what your Hiring Manager had budgeted for, meaning that the Return-on-Investment (ROI) for this hire will be less than planned.

It has not yet become an Obstructive Catalyst but should be addressed before it morphs into one. Perhaps you'll speak with the Hiring Manager to make sure they are OK with the higher numbers. Will it affect their ability to hire more people later? Is the ROI still high enough?

Kaizen

Kaizen (改善) is a Japanese word that simply means 'improvement'.

For our purposes, Kaizen means continuous improvement - constantly improving our efforts to get closer and closer to the bullseye with our recruiting efforts to find that perfect candidate.

We will analyze and update our Canvas a number of times to take into account both Obstructive Catalysts and Latent Catalysts in an effort to find the best people.

Muda

Muda (無駄) is another Japanese word – it literally means 'useless.' As it pertains to lean theory, it refers to wastes encountered in the manufacturing and other processes. We will adapt this principle to the recruitment function.

5 Principles of Lean

There are five generally accepted principles that govern how 'Lean' is achieved. They come to us from the world of manufacturing. I will demonstrate how each of them applies to the world of recruiting, and how each fits into your Lean Recruiting Canvas where appropriate.

1. Value Discovery

Within the manufacturing world, identifying is a matter of defining the value your product is offering the customer. Value is created by the producer and is (hopefully) recognized by the customer.

In recruiting, this gets a little more complicated. Why? Because there are two 'producers' and two 'customers'.

The first producer is the company and here the job candidate is the potential customer. The company is providing value for the job candidate in the form of a job. In order for the customer (in this case the job candidate) to recognize value, a few things have to happen.

Firstly, the company has to know what it is and what is does. And the recruiter has to properly be able to convey this information to the candidate. We address this in the Company USPs chapter where we define what is unique about our company's offering. While technically, a Company USP involves defining what is of value to the company's purchasing customer, it also provides value to the job candidate because it shows them what value this employer will add to their lives and their career.

Our Role UVP section illustrates value to the job candidate by highlighting how the role and its benefits are tailored to the person who is most likely to be interested in this role. It is about alignment. We are providing the customer (the job candidate) with the value they seek. Both the Company USPs and the Role UVP are included in the job advertisement as a means of communicating this 'value.'

In the second instance, the producer is the job candidate, and the company is the customer. After all, the job candidate has a product to sell - namely their skills and abilities - which will help their customer (the employer) achieve their own goals. Value discovery becomes a bit more difficult here as job candidates largely don't realize they are involved in this process. How does a job candidate convey their value? How does a recruiter find it? From the job candidate's perspective, they are creating a resume and looking for a job. This is an imperfect process mainly because very few job seekers are experts at writing resumes, (which is really a personal marketing document designed to share value) or looking for jobs. In fact, the type of candidates you are ideally looking for – people who stay in jobs for more than a few years – will have even less experience than people who jump from job to job. Some people are experts at getting jobs, but not necessarily at staying in them.

Much of the value discovery of the candidate's 'product' is dependent upon the skills and abilities of the recruiter. How good is the recruiter at searching for value (Boolean search skills, referral programs, writing effective job ads) and then recognizing value (screening calls and general interviewing abilities)?

2. Mapping the Value Stream

Mapping the Values Stream involves mapping each of the steps necessary for the successful creation of a product from start to finish. It is important to highlight that manufacturing involves 'making' something. Recruiting is more of a searching and sorting process, a bit like mining for diamonds.

First you decide where to dig, then you find diamonds, and then you sort according to various desirable and less desirable qualities.

Mapping value in recruiting begins with the creation of your Lean Recruiting Canvas. Value is mapped for the company in a few different sections; Problem, Solution, Cost Structure and Value Added. In the Problem, we are identifying what business problem has been encountered that led the company to believe that they need to hire someone. The Solution identifies what the hire should look like fairly precisely. (This section also helps us identify when a new hire is not actually necessary to solve the Problem – how's that for value?) The Cost Structure and Value Added sections work together to help us determine the Return-on-Investment for the new hire, ideally in currency figures.

Value Mapping for the candidate, as discussed above, involves proper identification of the Company USPs and Role UVP. Once we have done this, we can move on to the execution of our active recruitment strategy.

For the recruiter, the most important steps are defining what the Ideal Employee will look like, deciding what Sources to use to find candidates, and the implementing the Process for finding, evaluating and hiring candidates.

3. Creating 'Flow'

Flow is the continuous movement of the Value Stream. If something goes wrong, flow is interrupted. This should be avoided at all costs. In the manufacturing world, interruption of flow can cause things like delayed delivery of orders, unhappy customers, and underutilized employees and machinery.

In the recruiting world, the interruption of flow can cause job candidates to accept offers with other employers (in the case of slow turnaround times between hiring steps), or delays in the company hiring the right person (especially if the hiring manager's and recruiter's expectations are misaligned).

The creation of Flow within recruiting relies on such factors as the skills and knowledge of the recruiter, the hiring process which has been created for a specific role, and also the establishment of key metrics.

The ongoing management of Flow within recruiting means systematically recognizing, and acting upon, Catalysts. A Catalyst is any factor that can hamper the flow of the recruiting process. It is also an opportunity to perfect the process.

Catalysts can be broken into two categories; Obstructive Catalysts™ and Latent Catalysts™. An Obstructive Catalyst is encountered when the recruiting process grinds to a complete halt, normally due either to a lack of suitable candidates or the rescindment of the job requisition. A Latent Catalyst occurs when the recruiting process slows to an unacceptable level (but doesn't stop) due to a number of possible circumstances. Latent Catalysts are normally discovered upon regularly scheduled reflection. Flow is re-established when Catalysts are resolved.

4. Establishing Pull

Establishing Pull in manufacturing refers to the process by which orders are pulled through a plant in order to meet demand by customers. A really good example of this is Amazon's print-to-order service. For example, if you purchased this book through Amazon, it didn't actually exist when you bought it. Amazon only printed it when you clicked 'Purchase.' Interesting, right? This is contrary to traditional

North American push manufacturing model whereby orders are produced based on forecasts.

The main reason why Pull is generally preferable to Push in manufacturing is that you don't have excess products sitting on shelves waiting for customers to buy them. Completed products tie up cash. And they might not sell, at least not at full price.

In the recruiting function, we do not have physical inventory. Our inventory includes the skills of job candidates and stored information (resumes, cover letters and notes). Still, the principles apply. After all, wasted time is wasted money.

So how do we achieve Pull? When we receive a job requisition, and all parties agree that a hire is required, we launch into an active search for candidates. This typically involves things like active Boolean searches across multiple platforms, the creation and publication of an effective job ad, and more. This is classic Pull.

More passively, however, we can be collecting inventory (job candidates and their resumes), without spending money on inventory, or a terrible amount of time. Remember, we have no physical inventory that requires financial investment – we are simply collecting and storing candidate information.

Good examples would be things like creating resume alerts, organizing hackathons and keeping attendee information for later, or attending MeetUps and keeping the details of potential future candidates. These passive techniques arguably fall under the Push category. We are however not 'pushing' all the way through the production line until we have an order. We are simply storing information for later use.

So how do we convert these techniques to Pull? Simple. Through Hybrid Sourcing™. Hybrid Sourcing involves the conversion of Push techniques to Pull results. Here are a couple of examples.

Let's say you have your resumes from your resume alerts automatically added to your Applicant Tracking System (Push). When you receive your requisition, you begin by searching through your ATS for these passive candidates and attempt to convert them to active candidates (Pull).

Or perhaps you have a paid employee referral program in place, which you set up last year (Push). Then, when you begin working on your requisition, you simply email relevant members of staff informing them that you have an immediate requirement, and also reminding them of the terms of the referral program and that you are once again actively seeking qualified candidates (Pull).

5.   Seeking Perfection

Perfection is the ultimate goal of Lean methodology. Can it be achieved? Maybe. Should we strive for it? Always. Recognize your stumbling blocks early, take action more quickly, and continue to set the bar higher.

With our Lean Recruiting Canvas, we have the built-in agility to help us continuously improve our performance. We also have a set methodology for recognizing, and acting upon, Catalysts (see above). Later in the book, I will show you how to set regular periodic checks (both weekly and longer term) to ensure that you get closer and closer to the bullseye.

It is important to note that not only is recruitment affected by internal processes like hiring process and accurate role definition, it is also impacted by factors within the greater company, the industry at large and the economy as a whole. These 'external' factors make it all the more important to regularly update your plan and take into account a shifting environment. After all, there is no point in hitting the dart board where the bullseye used to be.

8 Wastes of Lean – muda

Our five principles of Lean, and associated processes, are designed to improve productivity largely through the elimination of waste. There are eight wastes, aka muda, in Lean manufacturing. Let's have a look at how (and if) these apply to recruiting.

1. Defects

This is clearly a term aimed at manufacturing. So how can this apply to recruiting? In manufacturing, a defect is something that has gone wrong with the production of the product. A serious form of harm occurs when the defect is only noticed after the product has been sold. The worst realization of a defect is a product recall, which is terrible for a company's reputation. It makes news headlines, and not in a good way.

In order to draw a parallel with recruiting, we have to think about what our 'product' is, and how to determine when something is wrong with the it. As discussed earlier, there are two 'producers' in the equation namely the company and the job candidate. If there are two producers, then there must be two products. What does each of these 'producers' produce for the other?

Firstly, the company's 'product' is a job for the job candidate. And what are the possible defects? There are many. It could be insufficient pay, unachievable goals or targets or even the work environment. Many of these defects stem from an inaccurate description of the company or the role. To eliminate these defects, it is imperative to be accurate, honest and open when it comes to describing the job opportunity.

In recruiting, you can rarely change your product, but you can change how it is described so that your customer (the job candidate) can decide if this is a suitable product (job) for them. If not, you will have unhappy employees who will quit. They will also help spread negative publicity about your company. Your average length of tenure will suffer and hiring costs will rise.

So what 'product' do job candidates produce? It is actually themselves. Or more aptly, it is the skills and abilities they bring to the role and the company. One could argue we all have defects. In contrast, one could also argue that we are all extreme specialists. Either way, we need to ensure that the skills and abilities a candidate brings to the table match the role. If you have been in recruiting for any length of time, you will recognize this as 'role-candidate fit.'

So how can this go awry? In an ideal world, the candidate sees a job, recognizes the match, applies, gets the job, and everyone lives happily ever after. But this isn't always the case. Our job candidate defect can arise from a few sources. Firstly, they may be overestimating their abilities. Or inversely, they may underestimate their abilities. Finally, there can also be a certain degree of embellishment on the part of some job candidates. While it is normally the job of the producer to recognize and rectify defects, in this case it is up to the customer (the recruiter) to find defects on the part of the job candidate and eliminate (as opposed to fix) unsuitable candidates from the competition.

2. Excess Processing

Essentially, this refers to performing any processes that are not essential to the production of the product. In recruitment, this really refers to performing any steps in the hiring process which are not essential. For example, you may require all new employees to go through a behavioral assessment, which may be a good idea for sales staff, but really isn't normally necessary for software developers.

By making candidates go through unnecessary extra steps, you will risk losing them to competitors due to slow processes, or you may just convince them that you as a recruiter don't know what you are doing. Not only must we include all necessary steps in the recruiting process, we must also ensure there are no unnecessary steps.

3. Overproduction

Making too much of anything is a bad thing. This harks back to our Push versus Pull production. If you push, you will invariably end up with too much product that you can't sell, at least not at the price you want.

In recruiting, overproduction refers to running too many candidates through the hiring process, which means you have to reject more people. When you put someone through the process and they are unsuccessful, they are less likely to apply again. This can a have negative impact on your reputation. The exception to this is passive sourcing, which as discussed above, can be converted to active sourcing through a process called Hybrid Sourcing™. Using the method, candidates often don't realize they are even candidates until you begin the active search, meaning you are mitigating the chances of negative sentiment being directed toward your recruitment process. Also, overproduction is quite frankly a waste of time and productivity on the part of the recruiter. They could be performing other tasks.

4. Waiting

Waiting refers to waiting for the previous step in the process to be completed. In recruiting, this refers directly to wait time between the steps of the recruiting process. This can be mitigated by getting the hiring manager to agree with, and committing to, each step and the associated time frames. If the hiring process takes too long, candidates will find other opportunities with companies that hire more efficiently.

5. Moving

This is one muda that may have no direct correlation to recruiting. Moving (sometimes referred to as Transportation) refers to the time wasted in moving parts or products from one place to another. You could argue that this applies when you have a candidate do a remote interview, rather than in in-person interview, but it is a stretch. As far as recruiting goes, Moving is really a subset of Waiting.

6. Inventory

In manufacturing, holding unnecessary inventory is an expense. Would you rather have money tied up in spare parts on a shelf, or would you prefer to have it sitting in your bank account? In recruiting, this is not so much a problem. Any passive candidates are simply added to our database until the time comes. The cost in doing so is minimal.

7. Motion

Motion refers to the unnecessary motion of machinery, people and even information. In manufacturing, this normally has to do with an inefficient layout of the plant floor. In recruiting, there is no plant floor. However, Motion refers to the steps in your recruiting process which we of course cover in the Process section of this book. We need to think about what steps, and in what order, are required to hire the best candidate possible taking into account a number of factors. Unnecessary steps are a waste.

8. Non-Utilized Talent

Slack in the manufacturing process results in people being underutilized or being utilized in a less than optimal way. In recruiting terms, this refers to the recruiter's time not being used in the most effective manner. They could be doing other high-value tasks such as onboarding, annual assessments or even recruiting for another role.

Recruiting Muda

While the standard wastes of Lean (muda) are useful for analysis, some of them are a bit of a stretch or don't work at all for the recruiting function. Below is a list I have created to better suit the recruitment function.

1. Lack of fit

In essence, 'fit' means the alignment of the job (and by extension the goals of the company) with a candidate's skills, abilities and personal goals. Does the job match the person, and vice versa? If there is a good fit, the company will have a productive employee for a long time. The employee will feel challenged, rewarded and fulfilled. If there is a misalignment of fit, employees are unhappy, underproductive and my even damage morale for other employees. The company will not get the return-on-investment they hoped for. With fit, we need to strive at all costs to make sure we have a match through both proper role definition, and appropriate and accurate candidate selection and vetting.

2. Waiting

Having to wait too long between steps will be the death knell of any recruiting drive. The most common form of this is having to wait for feedback from hiring managers, who may not realize that talent disappears if candidates are not processed quickly enough. Recruiting is a competition – a competition against all competing jobs and companies. If you wait too long between the steps of your hiring process, you will have to settle for second-rate employees.

3. Unnecessary hiring

Hiring someone who is not required in order to fulfill company goals is of course wasteful from a financial perspective, but it is also wasteful from a morale viewpoint.

Too many people hanging around doing too little changes the culture of the organization, and not for the better. In addition, hiring someone on a permanent, full-time basis, when a part-time contractor or consultant may be more suitable is equally as wasteful.

4. Opportunity of cost

Within recruitment, this refers to the tasks the recruiter could be doing other than recruiting. If your recruitment function is not slick and effective, too much time will be taken up by the recruiter filling requisitions. This time could have been used completing other high-value HR-related tasks, such as onboarding, learning and development, annual assessments, and of course recruiting other employees. The cost incurred is losing the opportunity to complete higher value tasks.

5. Poor hiring process

One-size-fits-all hiring processes do not work. Each type of job needs to have its own process, based firmly on the requirements of the role. Searching for, interviewing and assessing people for skills and traits that are not required for the role are a waste.

Also, unnecessary or superfluous steps in your hiring process gives candidates the impression you don't know what you are doing. They will then be open to offers from competing employers.

2. THE LEAN RECRUITING CANVAS

You will need several blank copies of the Lean Recruiting Canvas as you work your way through this book. We will fill it out a number of times based on a single job requisition you are working on. Don't expect it to be perfect the first time. The point is to get better as you progress. Be ready to track that progression, even if just for yourself.

You are welcome to refer to the Lean Recruiting Canvas on the next page. You can download a clean, full-sized copy of the Lean Recruiting Canvas by going to:

http://canvas.JustInTimeRecruiting.com

Lean Recruiting Canvas

Role:

Problem	Solution	Company USPs	Role UVP	Ideal Employee
	Key Metrics	Process	Sources	

Cost Structure	Value Added

CRAIG E BROWN

What is the Lean Recruiting Canvas?

The Lean Recruiting Canvas is a one-page strategy document that allows you to plan, execute, and continuously improve your hiring process for one specific type of role. That's it.

It could be for an iOS Developer, or an Inside Sales Representative, or maybe an Administrative Assistant. It doesn't matter the type of role.

One very important thing to remember going forward is that the Lean Recruiting Canvas is not intended to give you all of the answers.

It is designed to ensure you ask all the right questions.

What is the process for recruiting using the Lean Recruiting Canvas?

You will complete the Lean Recruiting Canvas a few times over the course of this book. This is so you can actually see your own improvement as you progress. And, that's the Kaizen component.

The process discussed in this book is identical to the process you will use in the real world. We'll take it slow initially, to make sure you get things right. Best to get things right now, then to have to correct them later!

Step 1 - Make a plan. This will take up the next ten chapters of this book as we go through the Canvas in detail.

Step 2 - Execute on your plan. No point in getting all dressed up for nothing.

Step 3 - Adjust plan for both Obstructive and Latent Catalysts. Strive for perfection.

Step 4 - Analyze your results to help with future similar hires.

What will you need?

You will need to have at least one job requisition with you. Ideally, it will be for a role that you are working on right now. If that's not possible, then choose a role that you frequently have to hire for, or perhaps one you typically have trouble with.

You will also need a few copies of the Lean Recruiting Canvas as indicated earlier.

What examples will we use?

With each of our Canvas sections, I will either directly discuss, or allude to, three different types of roles. The reason for choosing these roles is that they are all very different, and, with a bit of luck, you should be able to draw parallels between these and the roles you are working on.

Example Role 1: iOS Developer

This is a role that focuses on hard skills, where candidates largely either have the experience and qualifications, or they don't.

These kinds of roles are usually binary in nature. You either have a degree in computer science, or you don't. You either have three years' work experience, or you don't. Of course, candidates have to be interviewed for softer skills, but the hard skills remain most important.

Other roles that would fall into this category would be most engineering, accounting or science/research-based roles.

Example Role 2: Inside Sales Representative

This role focuses mainly on softer skills, like the ability to persuade people. There are, of course, technical elements as for most jobs today, but the softer skills remain most important.

The challenge with these types of roles is that behaviors are more important than 'hard' skills or accomplishments. There is no specific educational path for a sales person. It is often even difficult to check the quality of someone's past work.

The things we really need to find out about, people skills and motivation, have traditionally been very difficult to measure in any meaningful way. Almost any client-facing role would be similar. Think Management Consultants or Account Executives. Even Retail Sales or Customer Service Representatives.

Example Role 3: Administrative Assistant

Our first two examples, an iOS Developer and an Inside Sales Representative, are the types of roles that generally have to be headhunted. The recruiter will need to go out into the marketplace to find candidates that are qualified. If they are any good, they don't have to apply for jobs. Jobs come to them.

Hiring for the role of Administrative Assistant is quite different. If you post a decent job advertisement online for this type of role, you can expect to get upwards of 100 applications in a week. That's a lot of resumes to get through.

You could just hire the first good candidate that comes along. That's what many people do, including your competitors. But wouldn't you prefer to hire the best out of the 100? The problem is it can take a great deal of time and effort to get through a pile of resumes, even before the interviewing. It is difficult to justify using that amount of time when other work needs to be done. I'll show you how to reduce the time-to-hire, while at the same time ensuring you choose the best person quickly in the shortest time possible.

Other roles that fall into this category would largely be any that include the word 'assistant'. Roles like such as Marketing Assistant, Retail Assistant, etc. Most unskilled labor jobs would fall under this category as well. You get the point.

The Role Spectrum

The three examples above are fairly extreme in that one requires mostly hard skills, one requires mostly soft skills, and one will attract a ton of candidates, many of whom will be suitable. I have chosen these for illustrative purposes to make clear points on each.

The reality is most roles fall somewhere in the middle. As a result, you will have to choose which hard and soft skills to focus on when deciding what your Ideal Employee will look like.

For example, an ideal Psychiatrist would require a few different skills. First of all, they would need an advanced degree in psychiatry. This is a hard skill that can be easily found on the resume, and you wouldn't be able to hire someone without it. I would also argue that a good Psychiatrist also needs advanced active listening skills and the ability to be respectful[9]. These are both soft skills that seem necessary for this type of role.

A different example would be hiring an accountant for a 'Big Four' accounting firm. Not only do they have to have a degree in accounting, which is a hard skill, but they also have to have people skills because they will be working directly with clients. Being a consultant of any type requires certain personality traits, such as being a team player and having good time-management skills[10].

As a final example, consider the role of Retail Sales Representative. Like our Administrative Assistant, if you advertise a job like this, you will get a ton of applicants. But rather than primarily measuring hard skills, we will be more interested in measuring softer skills such as empathy and good problem-solving ability[11].

---

[9] https://www.psychologytoday.com/us/blog/shrink-rap-today/201201/what-makes-good-psychiatrist

[10] http://thinklikecenter.com/consultant/10-winning-qualities-of-a-consultant

[11] https://harver.com/blog/7-personality-traits-of-an-awesome-retail-candidate-and-how-to-assess-them/

Your First Canvas

Ready to dive in?

As a warm up exercise, I would like to you complete your first Lean Recruiting Canvas based on a job description you have on hand. I know you don't have a ton of information yet, but that's the point. You will see your progression as we go through this book.

No one will see your first attempt but you. Keep it for posterity's sake. Version 1.

If you haven't already done so, now is the time to download and print three or four copies of the blank Lean Recruiting Canvas...

http://canvas.JustInTimeRecruiting.com

Right, you've done that now? OK. Next, I'm going to walk you around the various sections of the Canvas and give you a very brief explanation of what section entails.

And then I'd like you to have a go at it.

Problem Section

So, the Problem. You've just been handed a requisition that you need to fill it. Write down what you think the Problem is. Bear in mind that this is the Problem the company is experiencing that needs to be resolved by this hire and, not the recruiting problem.

Solution Section

Write down the Solution to the Problem from the first point. Don't worry if you think you haven't got it right. This is just a quick exercise to show your progression over time.

Company USPs Section

USP stands for Unique Selling Point. Sometimes you'll also see things like Unique Value Proposition. This is asking 'What's so great about your company? What's unique about it? What differentiates it from its competitors?

Role UVP Section

UVP stands for Unique Value Proposition. Ask yourself, what's so great about this role? What makes it unique? What differentiates it from all the other similar roles that a job candidate will see online? What will make them apply?

Ideal Employee Section

This is your opportunity to jot down what you think would make the Ideal Employee for this role. Stick with three or four key points.

Key Metrics Section

Decide what you need to track. What do you need to measure to ensure that you're doing a good job recruiting someone for this role?

Process Section

That is, of course, the hiring process that you will take when you're recruiting someone for this role.

Sources Section

Where do you plan to actually find good candidates? How do you go out there and get them? How do you get their attention?

Cost Structure Section

Cost Structure would be things like how much will it cost your company to recruit a new employee. And, how much would it cost your company to employ them on an annual basis once they get the job.

Value Added Section

Value Added is the value the position will add to the company. Ideally in dollar figures or other currency figures – we're looking for a numerical value here ideally.

Tip: Your Value Added should be more than your Cost Structure or why would you be hiring them?

Take five or ten minutes to fill out your first Canvass based on the requisition that you have on hand. If you can't fill out everything, don't worry. We haven't done that much yet. What we're really trying to do here give us a baseline to measure your progress against as you move through this book.

Once you're done, put your completed Canvas to the side.

Now that you've had your first attempt at the Lean Recruiting Canvas, we're going to examine each square on the canvas in greater detail in the next ten chapters.

.

Problem: What Challenge is Your Company Facing?

A good place to start, I think, is the Problem, which will be your starting point on the Canvas 90% of the time.

Your Problem is a clear statement of the business challenge leading to the role.

How do you define a Problem?

Now, I would assume that many of you would have thought that your problem is, "I need to fill this role, because someone has left, or someone quit, or was fired," or whatever the case may be. But we're looking at the Problem within the greater context of the entire business, rather than just within the recruiting function itself.

I began working with Tom about three or four years ago[12]. He is the VP of Sales, and by default, the Chief Operating Officer, of an advanced software start-up based out of Toronto. The company makes a CRM solution that specifically focuses on the finance industry.

---

[12] Identifying details have been changed to protect privacy. All anecdotes in the book are written with the express permission of the participants. Except for Willy - never saw him again.

He was looking to hire a senior level software sales executive in the Boston area. For those of you who are not familiar with Boston, it has a robust financial district and it's a very good hunting ground for start-ups in the financial services industry looking for new clients. And it's not terribly far from Toronto either. It is very easy to get back and forth.

So, I went through my regular process at the time. I set up a meeting with Tom to really grill him on the company and on the position. We went through what he thought an ideal hire would look like, the salary, and all sorts of other requirements.

The next step for me was to request to have a demo of their software. I do this regularly with new clients that I work with so that I will have a good grasp of what I'm talking about when I explain their solution to prospective candidates.

I had a look at the software. It looked great to me and I was excited to start working on the requisition.

I started the search and fairly quickly found a number of candidates that I thought were pretty close to the mark. I sent them across to Tom with my notes. To my surprise, all of them were rejected, but for different reasons.

Three of the candidates were more-or-less on the mark. Their salary requirements were on target, but they weren't quite experienced enough.

I had another two candidates who were on the mark with regards to their type and level of experience, but unfortunately their salary requirements were too high.

Senior level software executives tend to command a pretty healthy salary. Normally in the US, their base salary will be in the range of $100,000 a year if they have five to ten years' experience. And then, if they're hitting their targets, they'll also earn another $100,000 a year, making their earnings at least $200,000 and sometimes higher.

The candidates that I had sent to Tom that were salary-appropriate only had about five or six years of experience, and he was really looking for nine or ten. The ones that did have nine to ten years of experience were all expecting an annual base salary in the $125,000 to $130,000 range, doubling that number with their commissions.

The great thing about working in major cities such as Boston, New York and London is that they have very vibrant business communities. The downside, of course, is that the salaries tend to be higher than employers expect (and hope for), especially in bullish economies.

After a couple of weeks of going back and forth with Tom and the candidates, I decided to have a heart-to-heart with him. I requested a second meeting, where we could hash things out and really see if we could make some adjustments to his requirements.

During the meeting, it became apparent the reason that Tom needed to hire salespeople was that his company had recently secured Series A funding for about $2M. When investors invest that sort of money in a company, they often do not 100% understand the technology. They are investing in the marketing plan. And by marketing, I mean sales.

In their marketing plan, they had indicated they were going to double their sales in the next six months and triple them by the end of the year. Tom determined the best way to do that was to get more salespeople onboard.

Tom had brought in over a million dollars in the last year by himself. His rationale was that if he could hire another senior level software executive, it would be well worthwhile, even if they were getting paid $200,000 (including their commissions). The new hire would bring in another million, so it's a five-to-one Return-on-Investment, which would be pretty good.

I went over my concerns with Tom at great length. It's not that the candidates couldn't be found. They were there. But they either weren't experienced enough or they were too expensive, so a change had to be made.

I started to talk to Tom more about his average working day and how much he was actually spending on various activities. He roughly divided it into three.

One-third of his day involved making his sales calls to new prospects, one-third involved following up, doing demos and closing the sale. The final third was concentrating on the rest of the business; everything from a wide range of operational duties, to fundraising, and emptying the garbage can.

It finally occurred to me that perhaps Tom didn't need another 'him' on the sales front. He didn't need to replicate himself, at least not at this stage. Perhaps what he needed was somebody lower down the chain to actually just make the phone calls for him and put his own time to better use.

For those of you who are not familiar with software sales, the entry-level role is often a Sales Development Representative (SDR). It can be critical depending on the structure of the sales department.

What SDRs do is mainly 'dial for dollars.' Their sole mission in life is to call prospects, either ones they've identified online or perhaps through lists that have been handed to them. They then try to get the prospect on the phone, explain the basic concept or solution, and then set an appointment on behalf of the senior software sales executive, at which point the more senior sales person would take over.

The great thing about SDRs is they free up the time of the senior people, and they also cost a lot less. Rather than looking at paying this person $200,000 a year with commissions, the base salary would more likely to be in the $40,000 to $60,000 range, with On-Target-Earnings (OTE) of approximately $80,000 to $90,000. So effectively, what we determined is that we could double Tom's value to the company – double Tom's sales – by adding a person who would cost less than half of what he expected.

In the end, we managed to find Tom an SDR who came on board very quickly. Sarah was a young university grad who had just under two years' relevant work experience under her belt. She was smart and driven and had done similar work for her last employer. Sarah managed to dial anywhere between 50 and 100 prospects a day. By the end of month five, Tom's sales had managed to double, and he was paying the new employee less than half of what was anticipated.

Our Problem wasn't that Tom needed to hire a new senior software sales executive.

Our Problem was that the company needed to double sales by month six in order to fulfill its commitment to investors. And we found a creative, cost-effective way to achieve that.

Remember what I said about Lean? We should only make changes if the result is an exponential improvement?

So the moral of the above story is that I should have grilled Tom more thoroughly at the outset. I had been somewhat reticent in doing so. I didn't want to pry.

But, had I done so earlier, it would have saved me a number of hours (maybe nine or ten) over a period of three weeks. It would have also saved Tom time. We got there in the end, but it would have been better if we had identified the true Problem and its associated Solution to begin with.

Identifying Your Problem

Really, depending on what type of organization you work for, the real Problem will arise from a need to do one of three things: to increase revenues, to reduce outgoings, or to improve efficiencies.

For-Profit Organizations

If you are a for-profit company, corporation or business, the most important factor to consider is increasing revenues. Sure, you will also be influenced by the reduction of outgoings and the improvement of efficiencies as well, but your primary concern will generally be to increase revenue to improve shareholder returns. It all comes down to the bottom line.

Public Sector Organizations

If you work for a public sector entity, you probably will not be as concerned with increasing revenues. Your revenues come from taxpayers. There's not really much you can do to increase revenues - you get what you get. Your goal, for a public sector entity, is to provide the best service possible to your clients, aka taxpayers, with the budget that you have been handed. You're focus will instead be on reducing outgoings or improving efficiencies as a means of doing this.

Charities and Non-Profits

A third example is if you work for a charity. You will be very interested in increasing your revenues through donations, and you'll be interested in improving efficiencies, but not so much at reducing outgoings. When you increase revenues, your goal isn't to keep that and give it to shareholders. Your goal is to give that to the clients of the charity. So the more you increase your revenues, the more you're going to increase your outgoings. The outgoings aren't so important to you to keep down.

With a charity, your main focus when defining your Problem will likely be how to improve efficiencies, or perhaps how to increase donations. Large charities have professional fundraisers for a reason – they bring in far more than is spent on their salaries.

Resisting the Temptation

Now, the temptation, which I'm sure many of you encountered when filling out the Canvas the first time, is to write down something like, "I need to hire because someone quit / got fired / got promoted / is on maternity leave."

Whatever the case may be, I'd really like to stress that needing to hire someone is a recruiter's problem, and not the business' Problem. The business' Problem is the problem that arose that led someone to think that, "We need to hire someone."

This is a really important point.

Be sure you do not confuse the Problem with Solution. Needing to hire someone is never the Problem. Hiring someone is a potential Solution. Not always, but we're going to get into the Solution section a little bit later.

You may be intimately familiar with your business. Maybe you've been there for a number of years and you know the specific department that's asked you to go ahead and fill this requisition very well. But, then again, maybe you don't. You may have to ask. You might want to start with your own recruiting team. You may have to go to the Hiring Manager.

If you do, you'll probably start by asking, "Well, how did the need to fill this role come about?" They're probably going to hit you with, "Well, someone got fired / promoted, so we have a vacancy." But you want to dig deeper to the root cause of the Problem.

As a general rule, dig until you see dollar signs.

I want to give you a couple of example business Problems, because this might still be a little bit fuzzy in your mind.

Example Problem 1

The first example is a software product company that sells its own software. The company has inbound leads that are not being followed up on and is losing $450,000 per year.

The term 'Inbound leads' refers to sales leads acquired through online activities such as being active on social media or perhaps through advertising. Potential customers express an interest in your product by completing an online form and submitting their details.

In this case, the company's Problem is that it has so many leads coming in that the current staff can't possibly pursue them all. Sure, it would probably cost between $50,000 and $75,000, or maybe even $100,000, a year to hire someone to follow-up on these leads. But, if the company spends this, it could receive almost half a million dollars in new income. That certainly sounds like a genuine business need.

Example Problem 2

"With the departure of one of our developers, we will not meet our project deadline, thereby endangering our contract with our client."

It's difficult to put a precise figure on this. It is possible that the client will be happy anyway and could even agree to extend the deadline. But the cost could really be that the next time this client needs to contract a company, they may think twice about choosing you because they think your company is too short-staffed. This sounds like a genuine business Problem as well. It's a little bit harder to quantify, but it definitely seems necessary.

Example Problem 3

"Our Administrative Assistant is going on maternity leave, thereby leaving our CEO unable to do her own job properly."

Again, this sounds like a genuine business need, because if the CEO, who's probably paid a lot more than the Administrative Assistant, gets stuck doing secretarial duties, she won't be able to make the more important decisions that are a much greater value-add for the company as a whole. I'd say this is a genuine Problem.

Why fill this role?

You need to step back from the situation you are in and ask yourself, "Why is it necessary to fill this role?" And, the answer should never be "because someone quit".

The answer has to be a genuine business need, or Problem. If you can't answer it in these terms, ask someone else for their opinion, someone on your own team or even the Hiring

Manager. If you dig deeply enough, you will come up with your Problem.

But if you can't think of an answer, then perhaps there is no Problem.

Here's a quick example. A salesperson leaves a company and the VP of Sales says, "We need to hire a new salesperson." You discover the reason the person has left is because the market has dried up a bit. The company is going through a dry spell, which is anticipated to last for six months to a year.

Maybe hiring nobody is the Solution in this situation, and that's actually a real win for your company, because you're saving a whole bunch in salary until the market rectifies itself.

If you are really struggling to find an answer to this question, if you are really stuck, ask yourself this…

"What bad things will happen to the company if this role is not filled?"

If neither you, nor the Hiring Manager, can answer this question, you don't need to hire someone.

Why examine the Problem in the first place?

As I just mentioned, you may not actually need to hire someone. You can save your organization thousands of dollars per year, maybe more, if you can find even a couple roles a year that you really don't need to hire for.

And it's not just about money. Yes, you're saving money, but you also don't have extra people hanging around with not enough to do. Morale will suffer. People will become bored. They will quit anyway.

You may come up with more effective alternatives. Again, I'm getting a bit ahead of myself with the Solution section, but hiring a full-time salaried employee isn't always the answer.

The best reason for examining the Problem thoroughly?

Quite simply, it gives us a clear and accurate starting point for filling your role.

If you go back to the root cause, the root Problem, this is going help you decide who exactly you need to hire to solve this issue. And all of the other points of the Canvas will flow so much more smoothly with an accurate Problem definition.

Problem Examples

I thought before we push through to the next box on the Lean Recruiting Canvas, I would share a couple of examples with you.

One will be for an IOS Developer, one will be for an Inside Sales Representative, and the third will be an Administrative Assistant[13]. I've chosen these three roles for very specific reasons which I outlined earlier in this book. But, in short, I chose the iOS role because it primarily involves looking for hard skills. The sales role involves assessing soft skills. And the Administrative Assistant role lets us examine a requisition where there will be a ton of applicants of varying quality.

iOS Developer

The Hiring Manager, who is the company's CTO, has come to me. He says, "Look, we need to hire a new IOS Developer quickly." So I immediately start thinking, 'Why? What is the business reason for hiring an iOS Developer?"

---

[13] If you would like to see completed copies of these example Canvases, you are welcome to download them here...
http://canvasexamples.JustInTimeRecruiting.com

I then do a bit of prodding. I talk to a colleague who is more familiar with the situation, and they tell me that our IT department is nervous about a project they're working on for a client. They're afraid that not having an iOS Developer will adversely affect their relationship. The team has back-end developers, a front-end Web Developer, and they even have an Android Developer, but, at the moment, they're short an iOS Developer. They need this person to complete the team.

Remember, 'needing to hire someone' is never the Problem, but it this situation does form part of the story and leads into the Problem itself. In this example, the Problem is that any delays in completing this particular project could result in bad relations with the client going forward, which in turn might result in losing the next big project, or the one after that. The team is concerned that the client could become reluctant to choose us in the future because we weren't able to complete this project on time.

I see that as a very legitimate Problem. I would probably write in the Problem box something like "Development team is worried that not Replacing iOS Developer will result in bad relations with client going forward - potential loss of income."

Inside Sales Representative

Now, we'll move over to the Inside Sales Representative role, and I'm going to use the Problem that I highlighted earlier in this book.

In this case, this isn't a matter of somebody having quit. The company is getting so many leads they actually don't know what to do with them. It's actually a good problem to have. They need to hire somebody else to meet the demand.

So here, the Problem, which is a very real business problem, is that the company is losing approximately $450,000 a year in revenue through leads not being addressed.

The leads are just disappearing. They're coming in. Potential clients are filling out forms online. They want their free demo. They want to talk to someone. We just don't have the staff to deal with it.

On our Canvas, we might write something like "Losing approximately $450,000 per year through leads not being addressed."

Administrative Assistant

In our final example, the CEO of the company has a challenge. Her Administrative Assistant has just gone on maternity leave. She has indicated to you that she needs a replacement.

For the last couple of weeks, the CEO has been covering her own administrative work, but she is finding it distracting. She is falling behind on the more important decision-making duties she is being paid for. At first, she didn't want a replacement as she wanted to keep the position open for the employee who is on maternity leave, but this is becoming more difficult as the weeks pass.

Looking for the root cause Problem from a financial perspective, you work out that the CEO's time is worth about $50 per hour to the company, while the Administrative Assistant is only paid $12.

Who would you rather have typing up letters? Someone who is paid $50 per hour or someone who is paid $12 per hour? This is a pretty solid financial case.

In the Problem box, you might write something like "CEO's time is being used inefficiently doing administrative tasks."

Your Canvas

So, at this stage, I'd ask you to get out a new blank copy of the Lean Recruiting Canvas and attempt to fill in what the actual Problem for your role. Version 2.

If you're not sure yourself, that's okay. Go find out. Find out from a fellow colleague who is also involved with recruiting and might be closer to the department that you're dealing with, or go talk to the department itself.

You're going to have to dig a bit, because, again, they're likely to say the Problem is, "Oh, somebody's left, and needs to be replaced," or something else that does not really define your Problem. You have to get to the root cause, and you have to explain to them why you are digging in order to shift their mindset. Keep digging until you see dollars and cents, pounds and pence.

So, go ahead. Fill out the Problem section of your Canvas now, based on the role you are looking at. I'll see you in the next chapter.

Solution: To Hire or Not to Hire

Think of this chapter as one giant sanity check.

Now that you have completed filling out the Problem for your specific job requisition, we're going to move on to the Solution. The Solution, quite simply, is a clear statement of an action that will resolve the Problem.

What will make your Problem go away permanently, or at least semi-permanently, maybe for a year or two years or perhaps longer?

If you only remember one take-away from this chapter, it is this...

Hiring someone is not the only possible Solution.

Somewhat counterintuitively, our first step is to think about how we can resolve the Problem without hiring someone on a permanent, full-time basis.

We've been asked to hire someone, but we want to think about really going back to our Problem again. How can we resolve this without bringing on a permanent, full-time member of staff?

I know. The most likely Solution will be to hire someone. After all, if we don't, this would end up being the last page of the book. Hire no one - Problem solved. Everyone go home. Turn the lights off on the way out.

I would say that your Solution 90% of the time will be to hire someone.

But - and this is a big 'but' - if you just briefly eliminate hiring someone as a possibility during the Solution brainstorming phase, it will help get your creative juices flowing.

You may think of ideas you hadn't considered before other than hiring someone permanently for a full-time position. Then, if you really can't think of any viable alternatives after having burned some brain cells, you hire someone.

I'd like to go through a couple of examples where hiring someone is not necessarily the best idea.

Example 1

First of all, maybe there's not enough demand to hire a new salesperson. Maybe things have been quite slow recently - no fault of the sales staff. If the market itself is slow in general, if there's a downturn in the economy, it can affect the company's performance.

Someone quits, so the natural instinct is to replace that person with a new hire. You approach the VP of Sales for a chat.

"Look, I know you're looking for someone new, but I also know things have been quite slow recently, and rumor has it, that's the reason why this person left. Why don't we put this hire on the back-burner for six months? I'll make an appointment with you, come back, and we'll re-address the issue and see if we need someone at that time once things have picked up."

Your VP of Sales will likely be pretty happy with that result because they have lots of other things to do, and they really don't want to spend their time interviewing someone else. In addition, they don't have to use their budget for the extra salary. That's a pretty good result.

Example 2

With maternity leave, the temptation normally is to hire a full-time contractor for the duration. But the issue with this approach is, even if this person is tasked with taking over all of the duties of the person who has gone on leave, they're usually going to be quite reticent about making the big decisions, particularly toward the end of the leave.

The reason for this is because when the person on maternity leave comes back, the contractor is not going to want to leave her with a bunch of decisions that she might think are not quite right, and just have to undo anyway. In practice, what normally happens when someone goes on maternity leave is the really important things that just can't wait are temporarily managed by a colleague who's already in place, and the other things that can wait, do wait.

Rather than hiring a full-time contractor, think about hiring maybe a temp to work ten or twenty hours a week, just to cover the administrative tasks, answer the emails, write the letters, that sort of thing. Put the projects that can wait on the back-burner, and hand off the projects that can't wait to another employee.

The benefit of this is that the person on maternity leave won't be worrying too much about their job. In most industrialized countries, these employees have to be taken back in an equivalent role. That doesn't necessarily mean it has to be the same role, but most want to come back to their own desk, to a job they know after having been away for so long.

Example 3

A third scenario you may encounter is you might get a Hiring Manager requesting to replace an employee because they have a use-it-or-lose it budget. They certainly won't tell you this is the reason, but it becomes apparent. They're afraid that their head count will drop. Even though they don't really need someone right now, they don't want their head count to drop because in six months or a year, they're going to need to raise it again. It's always much easier to justify replacing someone who has just quit, than it is to ask for an increase of headcount later.

I have actually personally been on the receiving end of this one myself. I lived in the UK for about a decade. I arrived in Britain in November 2001. If you know your history, that was a very uncertain time. No one was hiring. Even temp agencies had shut their doors. It was also a market I was new to and I was trying to learn the ropes. I was newly married and trying to get established. It was challenging.

I eventually got a job working in the public sector, specifically transportation. I was hired as a training manager. My job was to hire and then manage the work of three trainers initially and grow the department as demand dictated. My very first task was to hire the three trainers I would be managing. I was very excited.

On my second day, my boss, Jon, informed me that the budget to hire these three trainers was rescinded.

I was devastated. I actually couldn't believe it. Who would hire a manager when the budget to hire their subordinates was so precariously positioned?

I learned months later that departmental changes had been afoot for quite some time. Jon wanted to get his headcount up as padding for the future. He had hoped to get all four of us, but in the end, only managed to get approval for one. He hired me very quickly before this approval was removed.

While I was not a replacement for someone who left, it became very clear that hiring me was superfluous. This left me in a very strange situation I would never care to repeat. As a heavily unionized public sector employee, it was pretty much impossible to fire me. Great, you might think. But I literally had nothing to do.

I decided to make myself as useful as possible. I took over some duties of a colleague who was leaving, which involved checking machinery fault records. I won't get into it. Suffice it to say, it was more boring than watching moss grow. I dreaded Mondays. I was bored and the stress of trying to look busy was getting to me. My wife was worried about my health. I left as soon as I could get a new job.

It would have been far better if I had not been hired in the first place. Not only for my employer, but also for me. I could have gotten on with my life, rather than wasting time in a job I neither liked, nor was trained for.

The way you deal with this kind of situation is going to be up to you. However, I'll give you some tips later in the book on how to work effectively with Hiring Managers. Maybe it's something you want to challenge. Maybe the culture's open to that. Maybe it's something you can't really challenge. You get this sort of issue sometimes in public sector, and with very large corporates. It can become very political, so you will have to be careful how you deal with it.

The moral here is, don't hire someone if you don't need to. It sounds basic, but it happens all the time.

If you don't have to hire someone, you have saved yourself a bucket-load of time and lots of hassle. You've also saved your employer lots and lots of money, which, of course, you can bring up during your own next performance review.

Benefits for Agency Recruiters

In the Problem chapter of this book, I talked about how I convinced a client to hire a more junior sales person than they had planned for. It was better for their business financially as the salary was lower. And it was much more efficient.

Since I was acting in the capacity of an agency recruiter (as opposed to my work advising companies on hiring processes), I was taking a commission on the placement. By placing someone with a much lower salary, my commission had almost halved.

This might sound a little crazy. Who takes a hit like that? The simple truth is that if you act in the best interest of your clients by taking a short-term hit, you will win out in the long run. You have gained their trust. If you allow a client to hire someone more expensive than they need, it will backfire. Even if this person stays and contributes, your client will likely eventually realize their mistake. You will be associated with this mistake. At best, your client will think you are incompetent. At worst, they will think you led them down the wrong path intentionally.

So, to my agency recruiter colleagues, always go for the long play - it always works out in the end. You'll get more business because your clients know you are honest. And you will get referrals.

What are some alternatives to hiring?

I thought it would be useful to provide you with some alternatives to hiring permanent, full-time employees. This of course will not work all of the time. In fact, as indicated earlier, 'not' hiring will probably only be your Solution about 10% of the time. There will be some Solutions you have likely heard of before, and maybe some you haven't.

Hiring contractors or consultants

They usually cost more on an hourly basis but can be very handy for a fixed-term project. It could work out better than hiring someone on a permanent, full-time basis.

Outsourcing routine tasks locally or overseas

It really depends on the nature of the task, but generally you would only consider outsourcing a task if it is (a) fairly routine in nature and (b) not critical to your core business. There are lots of talented individuals who do this sort of work. If you assign work overseas, it will be cheaper, but of course the level of English may not be the same.

Offering overtime

Consider offering overtime to current employees when you experience a temporary surge in business. If you suspect that the surge is not permanent, then offering overtime is a simple way to meet demand. Also, you don't have to train anyone - they already know what to do. The flipside of this is that if this surge remains more-or-less permanent, it will actually become cheaper to remove the overtime and hire permanent employees.

Retraining current employees

Let's say one department is understaffed, while another is overstaffed. See if you can move people from one place to another. They may need training, but they have a number of advantages. First of all, they already understand, and have bought into, the work culture. Also, you already know they have a decent work ethic, and are smart and flexible. It's worth a shot and likely more cost-effective than hiring new people. It is also much better for morale than laying people off, and then hiring new people. You also won't have to pay severance packages if you live in a jurisdiction where this is the practice.

Hiring part-time parents

Some women choose not to go back to work full-time after their maternity leave ends. Increasingly, this also applies to men in jurisdictions where paternity leave is common. Although these parents do not want to return to full-time work, they sometimes want to get back into the work environment.

When the kids go to school, they have a four-hour window in the middle of the day, normally from about 10am until about 2pm, depending on school run timings. Often, these are highly educated people that can be employed at a reasonable price. Think about it.

Managing scheduling better

This is more for environments where shift work is predominant. Eons ago, I worked at a 4-star hotel in the

Rocky Mountains. It was my first real full-time job. I was a Bellboy, which largely involved taking luggage to guest rooms. Our shifts were normally split shifts from 7am to 11am, and then 3pm to 7pm. These shifts tended to coincide with peak check-in and check-out times. Since we all lived right on the hotel property, I just thought of it as a long siesta. Think about when your peak times are, and schedule accordingly.

Investing in technology

Consider technology for more routine tasks. You could use an automated phone tree for inbound calls, rather than a receptionist. You might even wish to implement an inbound lead capture system.

Hiring interns

Of course, you can hire interns. They often come to you cost-effectively. I would advise against taking on free interns. Free interns come with a certain degree of resentment. When you pay someone, there is a social contract that binds you. It tacitly stipulates that in exchange for money, the employee will put in some effort.

The downside with interns is that they lack industry experience and you will need to (and are probably obliged to) dedicate time to mentoring them. You may not want them to work on anything too important, because they are inexperienced, yet they have come to you because they want experience doing the important things. There needs to be a balance.

If you do hire...

If you do decide to hire someone, which is likely to be the case the bulk of the time, what do you need to write in the Solution box?

Let's keep it simple. Write in the job title and indicate that it is permanent, full-time. Then list up to three main activities the new employee will be working on. That's all.

Making Your Recommendation

First and foremost, what will make the Problem go away? Look to the left of the Canvas. Look at your Problem again. What will make that Problem go away more or less on a permanent basis?

You have three main options.

1. Don't hire at all. Why not? Money? Efficiency? You have found an alternative?
2. Hire, but not permanent, full-time. Consider contractors, temps, external agency help.
3. Hire permanent, full-time.

Solution Examples

Now that we've completed discussing our Problem and our Solution, I wanted to give you some Solution examples. Let's have a look at a few that I've come up with based on our example roles, which are the iOS Developer, the Inside Sales Representative and the Administrative Assistant.

iOS Developer

Let's start by quickly revisiting our Problem. Specifically, we have written, "Development team is worried that not replacing an iOS Developer will result in bad relations with the client going forward - potential loss of income." Simple enough. Very concise.

The first thing we want to ask ourselves is "What will put an end to this Problem, permanently?"

One option to consider, of course, is not hiring someone, or at least not hiring someone in the conventional sense. The team needs to fill the role, so not hiring someone doesn't seem to really be an option here.

We could hire an external agency that's familiar with iOS development. However, the client is likely to realize that we've hired an external agency at some point, and then they'll probably think to themselves, "We don't need these guys. Why don't we just hire an external consultant directly ourselves?"

We'll assume that the best Solution here is to indeed hire an iOS Developer on a permanent, full-time basis and start thinking about what we are looking for specifically in this role.

We'll need someone who has published multiple game apps. This will help initially, as we complete our important client project. Going forward, they will also be expected to learn languages new programming languages so they can work on other projects for clients. They will also be client-facing.

In the Solution box, I would likely write "Hire iOS Developer to work on current project. Learn new languages, work with clients".

Inside Sales Representative

Let's pop over to our Inside Sales Representative role and have a look at that. Going back to our Problem, we have stated "Losing approximately $450,000 per year through leads not being addressed."

We're going to hire a new Inside Sales Representative within six weeks who will be closing $20,000 in sales in his first month, rising to $40,000 a month by the end of month three, and that will get us to just about half a million dollars within the next year. That basically means hiring someone who can really hit the ground running and can plug that leak entirely within three months, so be specific.

There really aren't a ton of alternative options to hiring someone in this case. Sales people are part of a team, and it is difficult to outsource the work of a critical team member. Quality would suffer. This is a full-time hire.

So, in the Solution box, I might write "Hire FT ISR. Will sell $500,000/year from inbound leads."

Administrative Assistant

And finally let's have a quick look at our Administrative Assistant role. We'll get a little creative here. We have defined our Problem as follows, "CEO's time is being used inefficiently doing administrative tasks".

Fair enough. But remember, our Administrative Assistant is on maternity leave and will be coming back, ideally to her same job. The Administrative Assistant's job is effectively divided into three main components. The first part of her job involves acting as the company receptionist (let's say this is a smaller company). When she answers the phone, she then re-directs the call to appropriate party.

The second part of her job involves administrative tasks directly related to the CEO. She filters emails, composes letter/emails and acts as a diary manager for the CEO.

And the third part of her job involves organizing an office move. Things have been going well for this company, and they are bursting at the seams. They need a bigger space. It's a good problem to have.

For this Problem, we have a three-part Solution. Here it is. For the telephone answering, we will implement a call-answering service. These services normally only cost a couple hundred dollars a month and do exactly the same thing as a real employee. Someone answers the phone in your company name. After greeting the caller, the call is then directed to the appropriate person. If this person does not answer, the service takes a message, which is either emailed or texted to the recipient.

The office move will need to be handled by a current employee with good knowledge of the internal workings of the company (and the politics). Since this is meant to be completed within the next few months, we clearly cannot wait until our current Administrative Assistant returns from maternity leave.

For the administrative tasks that are directly related to the CEO, we will need to hire someone. But we can do this on a part-time, twelve-month contract for about four hours per day.

In this case then, the Solution box would read, 'Hire PT contractor 12-months to help CEO. Use service for calls, hand the office move over to Jack.'

Your Canvas

At this stage, I would ask you to go back to your own Lean Recruiting Canvas for the requisition that you have in hand and spend a bit of time filling out your Solution. Have a chat with somebody else in your department if you need to, and you can certainly go to the Hiring Manager and talk to them as well.

This is a really important box on our Canvas, so take the time to get it right.

Ideal Employee: Strive for Perfection, Simply

This chapter is all about simplification. We are going attempt to boil our needs down to three or four traits or experiences that our Ideal Employee should possess. Humans are incredibly complex, so this will be challenging.

The reason this chapter is called 'Ideal Employee,' rather than 'Acceptable Employee' is that we are looking for the best employee, and not just someone who will do in a pinch.

What Does 'Ideal Employee' Mean?

This may seem self-evident. In fact, the meaning is indeed self-evident, but the practice is not.

In the Ideal Employee section, you should write three to five bullet points that will aid you in the search for the perfect candidate.

These will be the key terms you will need to lock onto as you sift through dozens of resumes. In effect, we are also beginning to build our job ad.

Your three to five bullet points should be experiences or traits the candidate absolutely must possess in order to be considered for the position. The word 'must' is critical here. Unless the candidate has these three traits and/or experiences under their belt, you don't want to speak with them under any circumstances. This will take a fair amount of discipline, but it is worth the effort.

Hard Skills

A very simple example of a hard skill is insisting on a law degree when hiring a lawyer. Since having a law degree is a prerequisite for becoming a practising lawyer, it would be impossible to hire one without it.

Here's an example, however, that sits a little more in the gray zone.

Normally you would expect to see a Computer Science degree required for Software Developers. I'd say 80% to 90% of Software Developers will have this degree, and maybe even more. But, it is possible to set the bar too high. If the role is hyper-focussed on front end development, a degree from a technical college might just do the trick. If your technology team is open to the lesser degree, and the candidate can prove they can do the work, then it not only opens up the pool of candidates to include solid people that your competitors may not consider, but also could mean some cost savings as well.

In this case, your bullet would be...

- Bachelor's Degree or Associate's Degree in Computer Science[14].

---

[14] For the benefit of non-American readers, an Associate's Degree is simply a degree from a college, rather than a university.

Another alternative to a Computer Science Degree is a degree in electrical engineering. These two degrees used to be quite different, but today there is a fair amount of overlap. Any good degree-granting program in electrical engineering nowadays will have a strong software development component.

If you are willing to consider this, your bullet will be...

• Bachelor's Degree in Computer Science or Electrical Engineering

You may certainly also demand a minimum number of years' experience in lieu of a degree. I have never really had this work for hiring Software Developers, but perhaps you'll have better luck. The hesitation by employers comes from the candidate's knowledge base likely being too narrow, meaning the employee won't be able to work outside a specific sphere. They also are not likely to have experience in formal software architecture design.

In the previous example, we have looked at some hard skills, namely educational backgrounds. Let's have a look at a softer example.

Soft Skills

Soft skills are more relevant in roles where 'people' skills determine whether or not the employee is successful in their job. The challenge though is that they can be difficult to confirm. Most people will include things like 'team player,' or 'enthusiastic' on their resume as a matter of course. It's not that they are necessarily being dishonest – most people believe they are indeed enthusiastic and a team player. If you had a room full of people and asked everyone to raise their hand who is not a team player, very few would do so.

‌

So, why do we include them on our list of bullets if they are so hard to prove, especially since we cannot scan a resume for them accurately?

We include them because they are absolutely necessary. While we may not be able to *easily* search for these terms, we can certainly screen for them. We will get into this in much more detail in the 'Process' chapter.

As an example, Technical Sales People need to have a number of traits; some you might expect and some that you wouldn't. According to a study published in the Harvard Business Review [15], two of the top seven traits that top technical sales people share are modesty and lack of gregariousness. This surprises most people because when you hear the word 'salesperson,' many of us immediately conjure up an image of an unscrupulous used car salesman. But in reality, a top technical salesperson needs to be humble and won't mind not being the centre of attention.

I know this from personal experience. I have interviewed a ton of software sales candidates over the years. The braggarts never get the job. The ones who are advanced to the next stage of the interview process are generally modest, and very curious. They are never the kind of person who makes you feel like they are trying to 'close the deal.' They are generally the kind of person you can picture yourself grabbing a cup of coffee with.

So let's say our bullet point is....

- Modesty (teamwork required)

---

[15] https://hbr.org/2011/06/the-seven-personality-traits-o

THE LEAN RECRUITING TOOLKIT

Education Versus Experience

We tend to look for things that can be located easily on a resume. We might require an Administrative Assistant to have an Associate's Degree in Administration. But, is that really necessary? Probably not.

We chose it because it is easy to identify on the resume. We can even get our Applicant Tracking System (ATS) to automatically filter this for us. We are going to get a lot of applicants anyway, so screening out 80% of applicants based on this criterion makes sense, right?

Wrong. You may have very well thrown the baby out with the bathwater. Who's to say the best Administrative Assistant has a formal education in Administration? Maybe he has five years' experience and can type 50 words-per-minute with only a high-school education.

Also, a more formal education, such as an Associate's Degree, might indicate the candidate is looking for career progression and may not stay for the long term. For this type of role, you might decide that you are looking for a 'career' Administrator who just wants to put in their 9-to-5, and then go home.

As an HR professional, you may find it tough to accept this. You are trained to help all employees achieve their full potential, and progress. This is usually reinforced in annual performance reviews where we ask people what their goals are for the coming year, or five years. For some people, goals are just not work related. They want a cottage on the lake, or a vacation in Bermuda or a new car. To them, their job is simply a means to facilitate their other goals. It's not that they are miserable or have no ambition. It's just that they work to live - they don't live to work.

A friend of mine has been working at the front desk of women's residence at a university for over 20 years. She's good at it. She's happy.

In contrast, I already gave the opposite example where someone might want to consider a Software Developer with a certain number of years' experience, rather than a formal degree. You might get lucky, but I wouldn't recommend this route. A great Software Developer needs both deep and broad knowledge. Self-taught developers may have a deep knowledge in a particular area, but rarely a broad comprehension of multiple software languages, platforms, or full-stack development.

Never use 'or equivalent'

Never use the phrase 'or equivalent' in your bullets. For example, 'A University Degree in Marketing, or equivalent.' There are three reasons for this.

Firstly, it leaves too much open to interpretation to the candidate. As a result, this can lead to gender bias.

In a study published in the Harvard Business Review[16], the author first acknowledges a study conducted by Hewlett Packard whereby 'Men apply for a job when they meet only 60% of the qualifications, but women apply only if they meet 100% of them.'

The author then goes on to try to determine why this is the case. In her own study, she surveyed 1,000 men and women and asked them, "If you decided not to apply for a job

[16] https://hbr.org/2014/08/why-women-dont-apply-for-jobs-unless-theyre-100-qualified

because you didn't meet all the qualifications, why didn't you apply?"

Many of the responses were so close, they were statistically irrelevant. But there were two that really stood out, where women's responses were much higher.

1. "I didn't think they would hire me since I didn't meet the qualifications and I didn't want to put myself out there if I was likely to fail."
2. "I was following the guidelines about who should apply."

Women on average are much more likely to follow the rules when applying for jobs than men. According to the results of the author's study, most men (and yes this is a broad generalization) would look at the phrase 'or equivalent' and think, 'close enough.' Whereas most women will think to themselves, 'I'm probably not qualified.'

In other words, using the 'or equivalent' clause attracts applicants who overestimate their abilities. At the same time, it deters applicants who follow the rules.

The second reason to not use the 'or equivalent' phrase is that you cannot search for it. This is a really important point. Whether you are actively headhunting, or screening hundreds of resumes, you need to hold a few key points in your mind so you can compare quickly against each resume. An 'or equivalent' phrase means that while you scan each resume, you then have to mentally brainstorm all of the 'equivalents'. It's exhausting and time-consuming.

The third reason is that it is lazy. An 'or equivalent' phrase means that you couldn't be bothered thinking of the alternatives. So, give it some really good thought and be precise. It will be worth it in the long run.

Do not include 'nice-to-haves'

I have implicitly covered this point, but I think it is really important to hammer it home. Do not include qualities and skills that are 'nice-to-have' in your bullet points for the Ideal Employee box on your Canvas and do not include them on your job description.

Certainly, if you have two equal candidates, you could always choose the one who has that extra skill, but there is no need to try to anticipate what those extra skills will be and write them down. The first problem with this is we can be tempted to search / screen for this criterion and give it equal, or sometimes greater, weighting than our primary points. No one will care that your iOS Developer knows a little Java if he is terrible at coding in Swift, which is a primary iOS coding language. Leave it out.

The other problem we touched on earlier. Some people will self-screen themselves out of the running based on everything you list out in the job ad, even if they could have been very good at the main job requirements. Instead, you will get those who overestimate their abilities applying. Do you want to have a pool of interviewees who tend to overestimate their abilities? Nope.

Too tight? Don't worry.

I know what you are thinking.

'What if the bullets are too tight, so specific that they eliminate all the best candidates?'

That's OK. That's why our Canvas is Agile. We can loosen things up later if is not working out. But you must begin by setting the bar high and being precise. You have to set a course of action and pursue it. You can change it if necessary, but you can't change directions if you aren't moving.

Ideal Employee Examples

iOS Developer

With the iOS Developer, we're going to start by requiring them to have either a Bachelor's Degree in Computer Science or a Bachelor's Degree in Electrical Engineering. As I indicated earlier, either of those would normally suffice. We're not going to accept an Associate's Degree, however, because those tend to be quite tightly focused on one area of expertise and we may want this person to do other types of programming in the future as well. So, the Bachelor's Degree in Computer Science or a Bachelor's Degree in Electrical Engineering will be a must-have.

They also need to have a really solid knowledge of the Swift programming language. Swift really is the coding language of choice nowadays for iOS apps. Even just a couple of years ago, having a good knowledge of Objective-C was all that was required to build native iOS apps. Swift was, at that time, the new kid on the block, but it really has taken over as the primary coding language of choice.

Having object-oriented programming experience is also a must. Even if you may not have a background in software development yourself as the recruiter or only have a cursory understanding of what 'object-oriented' means, this is a must have that the employer has insisted on, so we'll include it.

And finally, candidates need to have multiple published iOS apps. The employer has insisted on this. You might think this is setting the bar quite high, but if we set the bar high to start with and things turn out to be a bit tight in the marketplace, you can always look at adjusting things later.

If we look at the requirements as a whole, we have a list of things that will get an iOS Developer onto your short list. These requirements will likely get them through the initial screening call and to the stage where they have to prove their coding chops; whether it is through an interview or a coding test.

These are also things that can fairly easily be found on a resume. You can very easily see if someone has a Bachelor's Degree in Computer Science or Electrical Engineering. You can also see if they have the word 'Swift' on their resume even if you don't know what level of knowledge they have. Just the word "Swift" is enough to scan for on your initial pass. Quite often, candidates will have hyperlinks to their published work embedded into their resumes, so with a bit of luck, these will be easy for us to discover.

So far, these are our bullets for this role…

- Bachelor's Degree in Computer Science or Electrical Engineering
- Great knowledge of Swift programming language
- Object-oriented programming experience
- Multiple published iOS apps

Inside Sales Representative

Our next example is for the Inside Sales Representative. We're going to look initially for a two-year track record of exceeding quota selling SaaS software solutions. We can go into the resume and verify the dates, if they have experience selling software, and what length of time that is. I like to go for two years. Most people insist on three, but two is enough to verify a track record. And if other recruiters are looking for three years, we might be able to scoop someone up at the two-year mark, rather than competing with all other employers who are looking for the magical three years.

With sales people, particularly in the US and Canadian marketplaces, the word 'Quota' tends to be a very good search/scanning term. Candidates who beat their quota tend to brag about it on their resumes. People who don't meet quota tend to leave it out.

Also, they need experience conducting online remote demos. Most people who have done this will put it right on their resume. It really is mandatory for most technical sales roles nowadays.

The final thing is we need is a team player. As previously discussed, almost everybody will put this on their resume. It's not something that we can verify at the scanning and screening stage. It's something that has to be verified later, so for now, we're going to just search and screen for the first two points.

Here are our bullets for this role…

- 2-year minimum track record of exceeding quota selling SaaS software solutions
- Experience conducting online, remote demos
- Team player - check modesty

Administrative Assistant

Then finally, for our Administrative Assistant role, we want the candidates to be able to type properly, so we're going to insist on 50 words per minute, error-free. It might be setting the bar a bit high, but why not? Like I have said, parameters can be adjusted later.

The candidates should also be very adept with the Microsoft Office suite. They should be able to use Word, Outlook, PowerPoint, and probably Excel as well.

And finally, they should be able to prioritize multiple tasks. Again, the first two bullet points we can probably find in a resume. The last one has to be verified later as most people will have this on their resumes, whether it is true or not.

I omitted any sort of formal education, because if they can do the first three things we have indicated, it is largely irrelevant if they have a Bachelor's Degree or an Associate's Degree. They can do the job, and that's what we're after.

Here are the bullets for this role…

- Type 50 words per minute error-free
- Strong ability to use Microsoft Word, Outlook, PowerPoint and Excel
- Ability to prioritize multiple tasks and work to deadline where appropriate

Your Canvas

Go for it. Write out your bullets. Keep it to three if you can, and no more than five. And remember, we only want to include things that are absolutely necessary to do the job. No 'nice-to-haves' or 'or equivalents.' If it doesn't fit in the box, you have too much.

Be precise. Be disciplined.

Company USPs: What Clients Want & Who Cares?

So far we've examined our Problem, our Solution, and our Ideal Employee. In this chapter, we will work out what our Company USPs are.

Let's first of all look at what 'USP' means. It stands for Unique Selling Point, or sometimes Unique Selling Proposition.

What does USP mean?

A Unique Selling Point is quite simply, "a feature of a product that makes it different from and better than all its competitors."[17]

In this chapter, our 'product' will actually be our company. Quite simply, we want to define what makes your company different from your competitors. That's all you need. While the definition above uses "different from and better than," I only used the word 'different' because different is usually

---

[17] https://dictionary.cambridge.org/dictionary/english/unique-selling-point

better, particularly if there is a large enough market, whether it is local, or global. If your product (or in this case, your company) is different from your main competitors, there will very likely be enough customers out there who like your difference - enough to keep you in business.

Why examine the USPs?

At this stage, you're probably wondering, "Well, why the heck are we examining this? We're in the business of recruiting job candidates, not in the business of selling our company's product. I'm in HR, not marketing."

There are two very good reasons for you to understand your company's USP's. First of all, when a candidate stumbles across your job description, or you reach out to them after a search campaign, the candidate will go away and look up your company online. They'll look at your website, your LinkedIn company profile and your Facebook page. They'll look to see if they can find you on Glassdoor. They will be trying to evaluate:

- Your reputation
- Your growth stability
- How many people work there
- How long the company has been in operation

Essentially, serious candidates will want to make sure you are viable and stable. They want to ensure that if they take a job with you, you won't go out of business six months later. As a result, highlighting your USPs is important, particularly with newer companies. It helps to prove that you have a viable product or service, and that you are here for the long run.

Secondly, candidates are trying to work out if your company or key messages are what they want to be professionally associated with. As much as we like to think that employees will stay with us forever, they rarely do. A career is a journey, and the path employees take have to make sense to them and look good to future employers. They will be looking for a clear message, which is where the USPs come in. Can they describe in 20 words or less what you do? Is it professional? Is it cool? Because when somebody at a party asks them what they do, they want to be able to say something like, "Oh, I work for Company X and they're the only manufacturer in the world of Product Y."

Snappy, right?

If it rolls off the tongue easily, it implies stability, strength and direction. If they can't explain clearly what the company does, then they're going to have a difficult time explaining it to friends, colleagues, customers, and future employers.

How to write it

When we identify our company's USPs, we ideally want to see a descriptors like, "first", "only", "biggest", "most" or "easiest." Superlatives clearly show people that you're the only one in the world, or you're the biggest one in the state or province, or you're the one who does something more than anyone else. These words tend to end in 'est' – biggest, easiest, fastest. Or have two words beginning with 'most' – most used, most visited, most viewed.

The best way to illustrate this would be to look at a few examples.

"Company A is the most flexible project management solution with best-practice templates and portfolio management dashboards on Sharepoint."

In this example, I am saying that I believe they have one of the very few bits of PM software that's built on Sharepoint, so that's pretty unique. And then they have their templates.

I'd say that's a pretty good descriptor. You'll note they have the word most in there. Perfect.

Here's another example.

"Company B - "The easiest way to pay your employees."

This company is a payroll solutions provider. Are they actually the easiest way to pay your employees? Who knows, but it's certainly a bold claim they now have to live up to. You'll note they use the word 'easiest.'

Now a final example.

"Company C is the only supplier of extra-large widgets in the tristate area."

In the first two examples, we're talking about global software solutions. But it doesn't have to be that way. It could be something fairly ubiquitous / local like widget manufacturing. As long as you highlight what makes you unique (in this case size and location) then customers will call you.

What not to say

I hear this all the time. You ask someone, "What's really unique about your company and what sets you apart?" And the response is, "Well, we have really great customer service."

Okay. Let's get this straight. It's fantastic to have great customer service, but it's kind of expected. And it's definitely not unique.

Everyone says this. It would be very odd for a company to say, "We have a great product and average customer service." People just don't brag about mediocrity.

Everyone will say they have great customer service, whether it's true or not, so this claim is not unique. Even if it is true and is a selling point, it's not a Unique Selling Point.

The other thing that happens when people describe their company USPs, is they list off all their Fortune 500 clients, or they'll talk about how many millions they've done in sales.

These may be your company's successes, but they're not what is unique about your company from a marketing perspective. Using this sort of descriptor is an attempt to show people you are a good supplier by virtue of your successes – it is the result of your USPs, and not a USP itself.

And, it's not what's going to attract a new customer, or in this case, an employee.

You have no competitors?

Some companies, particularly start-ups, will tell you that they have no competitors. It usually isn't true; they just haven't done enough research. If by some strange twist of fate they actually don't have anyone competing with them, then the 'status quo' is the competition. Most people don't like change. It's a pain in the butt. Your company offering has to be a great enough solution to force customers to abandon the status quo and dig out their wallets.

You have to think about what your company does that is strong enough to force people to buy from you, rather than doing nothing.

Having trouble?

If you are really stuck trying to work out what your Company USPs are, ask your sales or marketing department. They should - if they are any good - be able to rhyme it off easily. They will also be familiar with the terminology. Don't let them off the hook with 'We have great customer service." Grill them.

Ask them this. "When we get a new client, what specifically makes them choose us over a competitor?"

Company USPs Examples

iOS Developer

In our iOS example, we have already determined in the last chapter that we need to hire an iOS Developer so that our client continues to be happy with us and doesn't choose to go elsewhere.

Now we need to go back and examine what it is that we do as a company. We know that the development team is working on a project for a client that includes iOS development, Android development and some other things. When a company does a few different things, it can be hard to narrow down the USPs.

After talking to management and your salespeople, you learn that yours is actually the only company that provides integrated iOS, Android, web, and even Internet of Things (IoT) solutions in the whole of Ireland.

It may be a mouthful, but you're the only company who does it.

The type of client that would choose your company is a client that tends to do a variety of projects. Since they won't really know what's coming down the pipeline at any given time with their own clients or product lines, they'll want to choose a supplier that can handle a variety of projects, and make them all talk to each other. If somebody needs that sort of solution, chances are your company is going to get the call. It also turns out that they prefer to choose a supplier located in the same part of the world as them, in this case Ireland, so they can easily make an in-person visit if needed.

So, in our Company USPs box, we'll put "Only provider of integrated iOS apps, Android apps, Web solutions and IoT development in Ireland."

Inside Sales Representative

Our next example is the Inside Sales Representative. The company in this example creates business management software for chiropractic medical practices in the US, so the software is specifically tailored to the chiropractic industry.

Because the software has such a narrow focus and caters to specific type of medical practice, it's really an off-the-shelf solution. Very little customization or configuration is needed because it has already been pre-configured for chiropractors. In fact, it turns out that this company is the only creator of off-the-shelf business management software for independent chiropractic practices in the US.

There may be many companies that can create business management software for doctors, and there may even be many that are capable of creating business management software for chiropractors, but that software will not be off the shelf. It would need to be custom-built, and, therefore, will be considerably more expensive.

So, for this Company USP box, we'll write "Only creator of off-the-shelf business management software for Chiropractors in America."

Administrative Assistant

For the Administrative Assistant example, the company is a distributor of commercial and industrial lighting, which isn't necessarily that unique. There are probably a lot of companies out there that do the same time, but this company has a specific geographical patch.

The company is in the Midwestern states of America and is the largest distributor of industrial lighting in the Midwest. That's a very simple and strong USP. It would certainly dictate why our clients would want to use us as a supplier.

So, for this Company USPs box, you would write "Largest distributor of industrial lighting in the Midwest."

Your Canvas

At this point, you should return to your own Canvas for the role that you've been working on and fill in your Company USP, or USPs, or a combination of factors that make your company unique in the eyes of the marketplace.

Role UVP: Why Would Anyone Want Your Job?

We've already looked at the Company USPs and how they appeal to clients, thereby giving job candidates confidence and interest in our company. But now we're going to talk about the role specifically and how it appeals to job candidates directly.

What makes this role more appealing to candidates than similar roles with different employers? What will make a candidate get more excited about your job opportunity than those of other employers? Time to find out!

What's the difference between USP and UVP?

When discussing a company, we used the term USP. Now we are switching to UVP. If you do a search online, many, but not all, sources will use them interchangeably.

Jim Muehlhausen, author and founder of the Business Model Institute, uses a definition that makes sense for us. He states that "The unique value proposition (UVP) extends the concept of the unique selling proposition (USP) to include the benefits derived by the customer."[18] The customer in this case is the job candidate. And we are trying to 'sell' them the job.

With the Company USPs, we were focussed on the one thing, or combination of things, that makes the company unique in the world. With a role, however, we should look for a combination of factors that, although not unique in themselves, will make a unique (and hopefully irresistible) offering for a job candidate when brought together.

I'll first discuss the components of the job itself and how to make those appealing. Then we'll examine an area where we can really shine; benefits.

Both of these areas will be key components in your sales document, aka the job ad. We'll get into the creation of the job advertisement itself in more detail later in the book. To a large extent, the creation of a job advertisement is an exercise in copywriting. Although it is possible that you may need to implement a few new things, particularly on the benefits side, it is much more likely that you will simply need to focus on highlighting relevant responsibilities and benefits that are already in place.

Role Duties and Responsibilities

One of the first things that job candidates look for in a job advertisement is whether or not the role will be challenging. Not impossible, just challenging. Will it keep them intellectually occupied and stimulated? People like a struggle, but not an insurmountable one.

---

[18] https://www.dummies.com/business/start-a-business/business-models/define-a-unique-value-proposition-uvp/

A phrase like "You will be building a software solution fundamentally in C#" is accurate, but not particularly appealing.

However, phrasing such as "You will be working on, and implementing, a new state-of-the-art project with one of our largest clients," is much more appealing. It's exciting. It's challenging. And, it's something to spring out of bed for on a Monday morning.

Another thing that job seekers look for in a job ad is an indication that the role will be a step up from their current role from a 'responsibilities' point of view. Afterall, why would they want to take a new job just to do exactly the same thing that they are doing now?

Answer. They wouldn't.

Furthermore, they'll be looking to see if the work is important. Can they figure out for themselves how this role ties into the overall success of the company? People want to feel that their work matters. If their work is valuable, it will be easier for them to get raises and bonuses and advance their career.

I've had a few jobs in my day - I'm sure you have too - where I thought to myself, "Why am I doing this? It doesn't matter. I am making no difference whatsoever to the company or our clients."

Incidentally, it turns out that pay is not much of a differentiator. In fact, only 6% of people who change jobs do so for financial reasons.[19]

---

[19] https://recruitingdaily.com/7-big-reasons-people-change-jobs/

The most quoted reason for people to look for a new job is that they don't have the opportunity to fully use their skills and abilities in their current role. Give them this opportunity in your job ad. And when they come to work for you.

Benefits & Incentives

So now we'll move onto benefits as a contributor to our UVP. This is one area where we can really set ourselves apart from our competitors - not enough thought is usually given to this area. You can sometimes get a very easy win here.

When we think 'benefits', we often hear 'expensive'. But some of the benefits we can offer our employees are actually very cost-effective and can be ones that a lot of our competitors wouldn't think of.

We're first going to take into mind the stage of career that the applicant is most likely to be in. We'll examine a few options, both from an attraction and a retention point of view.

Importance of Demographics

To use one of my own examples, iOS Developers who know how to code in Swift are very likely to be under 35 years old. Not always, of course, but very likely. To be clear, we are not talking about what is politically or morally correct here, just what is likely. And again, whether it's right or not, most of them will be men. Hopefully that will change in the future but right now most iOS Developers who can code in Swift are men under the age of 35. So, you need to ask yourself what sort of benefits will be most appealing to them. Incidentally, if you are looking to attract more women to your development team to create gender balance, then you will need to think about what will attract them instead.

In contrast, if the type of role that you're looking to fill is for an experienced hire, such as a top - level software sales person with 10 years' experience, then you would typically be looking for someone a bit older. Someone with a family and kids. Someone who has a car and a mortgage. In this case, salary will be important to them, but so will other things. It can be important to bear in mind the most likely candidate's career stage when deciding what benefits to offer, or highlight.

Some companies will be looking to attract a range of ages, genders, etc. One creative way to appeal to a wide variety of employees is to offer a menu of benefits that will suit all. Employees can then choose the top three benefits that suit them. This can be a somewhat complicated, but it will certainly be worth it if it helps you get good hire after good hire.

Brainstorming Benefits

The types of benefits, especially more creative ones, will be a long list. Try Googling 'List of Creative Job Incentives' and see what comes up. Some of these you may have heard of. Things like gym memberships and onsite massages. One company I encountered even suggested offering house cleaning vouchers, which I thought was pretty unique. It certainly makes sense if your employees are very, very busy. In this case, the last thing they want to do when they get home on the weekend is clean their house. And, really, those vouchers wouldn't really even cost an employer much.

Let's break our employees down into two categories. There are certainly many more than this, but, for the sake of brevity, we'll look at new grads versus experienced hires.

New Grads

With new grads, I find base salary is usually more important than benefits. A high base salary gives them bragging rights among their friends, which can be quite important to young people.

On the benefits side, they don't really usually want or need many because they're young, they're healthy, and let's face it; they just don't have the kind of responsibilities that older folks do. New grads usually don't have childcare costs. They don't really have anything to insure at this stage because they don't own anything. One big exception would be in the US where health care is not free. But in Canada, in the UK and to an extent, in Ireland, healthcare is not a benefit that matters much because it is generally covered by the government.

You might want to instead think about the work environment you can provide to a new grad. It can be a quick win if you can offer an interesting office, especially if it's in a cool part of town. You'd be surprised how many people this would sway (including me). You can actually write on the job advertisement something like "Our offices have tons of light and space, being located in a converted factory in the old industrial district."

Amenities, sure. Snacks, why not? Dogs at the office. That's an interesting one. I've seen it before. But you should only really be offering this if you are trying to promote a casual and creative environment. It may not go down so well in a law firm.

Games room? I worked with a company a number of years ago that had installed a games room right in the office. The interesting thing was that although all of the employees bragged about it, it never got used. It was always more of a talking point. The CEO insisted it was worth it when recruiting, and also when speaking with the press. There may be enough value as a recruiting tool to have a games room, a gym or even a napping area.

And then we could get a little bit more creative still. How about a student loan payback scheme? If you're looking to hire smart young people, it stands to reason that not all of them are wealthy. Many of them will have massive student loans to pay back. If you can institute a student loan contribution payback scheme that attracts more smart kids than you currently are, that's a solid result. Here's how it works. Each full year that a new employee stays with you, you agreed to pay off $5,000 or $10,000 of their student loans. In effect, it is a bonus, but a very cost-effective one (talk to your accountant) that has the additional feature of encouraging young employees to stay with you for a number of years. It helps with your retention rate. How's that for Lean?

Experienced Hires

For experienced hires, salary is still important, but benefits become substantially more relevant than for new grads. Things like medical insurance, dental insurance, and pensions. As for other benefits you can offer them, some don't even cost that much. Flexible hours is a great example of this. If you expect them to start at 9am but their kids start school at 9am as well, why not let them come in at 9:30am or 10am and stay longer in the afternoon? As long as they're getting their work done, do you really care? If you do offer flexible hours, then it should be right on your job advertisement - it will attract attention.

Remote working is another example. This is great for mid-level professionals. I wouldn't try it with people who are in their first couple of years in the workforce because they are much more likely to need supervision and guidance. At the other end of the spectrum, more senior people are so expensive to hire that you really need them in the office supervising other people. But employees in the three to seven-year range are generally disciplined enough to work remotely, but not senior enough to be needed in the office every day.

Consider an education allowance. Most experienced professionals today realize that they need to continually update their skills. Worried they might leave after you train them up and take their new skills with them? Richard Branson has a nice take on this one. "Train people well enough so they can leave, treat them well enough so they don't want to."[20]

On the more creative side, perhaps think about an onsite daycare. If you have a lot of young parents working for you, that could be a real bonus that could tip people in your favor when applying for jobs.

Also think about a university contribution scheme for your employee's children. If they're mid-career, they're likely to be between 40 and 47-years-old and have children that are between 10 and 15 years old. And really, most people leave saving for university a bit too late. They're starting to think, "Oh my god, how am I going to pay for university?" It also means those employees will stick with you for years, at least until their children are done university.

When we create or emphasize benefits, we also need to think of the purpose of doing so. Some incentives attract, some retain, and some do both.

---

[20]
https://twitter.com/richardbranson/status/449220072176107520?lang=e n

Attraction Incentives

Attraction Incentives are the things that you will put on your job advertisement to encourage someone to click 'Submit.'

1. Medical and dental insurance. For more mature candidates, and some junior ones, this is a must for them to even consider the position. No one wants to worry about their health at work. It may not serve to retain employees, however, as most comparable employers will offer similar benefits.

2. Golden handshake. Giving employees a signing bonus in a very competitive market may work for you. It will not, however, keep them loyal. Include a clause that stipulates it will have to be paid back if the employee leaves before a certain period of time has elapsed.

Retention Incentives

1. Lunch. It sounds a little too simple to be of value, right? But, it can be a big expense for employees. Even at $10/day for a submarine sandwich, an employee could pay $200 per month just on lunches. Why would an employer pay for this? Well, $2,400 per year is no laughing matter. That's a vacation for a family. Covering this cost can help an employer retain people for longer.

2. While not technically an incentive, 'recognition' is an effective way to keep people on board. When people feel appreciated, they tend to stick around. Make your recognition program official. Give out trophies / medals where appropriate for a group project. Tweet it. Make a big deal of it. In more staid environments, congratulate the employee on a job well done, but make sure the other employees hear you say it.

3. Solid advancement program. Do people always get promotions and raises when they deserve them, or only when they ask for them? Formalize the process for getting a promotion. That way, employees will know what they have to do to get ahead (other than look for a new job). This also helps to reduce the gender wage gap as women are statistically less likely to ask for a raise or promotion than men.[21]

Attraction and Retention Incentives

This is the sweet spot. If you can come up with an incentive or benefit that will help you both attract *and* retain talent, now you are thinking 'Lean.'

1. Tuition payback schemes. This will turn the head of any young graduate with student debt. As already discussed, this benefit will have you contributing annually to helping employees pay back their student debt. It not only encourages more good candidates to apply for the job than normal, it will give them incentive to stay for the long term, because if they quit, they lose out.

2. More vacation days than expected. As discussed earlier in this book, the countries that have the most time off and the lowest number of hours per week at work, tend to also have the most productive work forces. Employees return to work refreshed and recharged. It works. Not only will this attract more candidates, but it will definitely make them think twice before jumping ship.

---

[21] https://www.bustle.com/p/why-is-it-so-hard-for-women-to-ask-for-a-raise-43454

3. Flexible working opportunities. Most intellectual work does not need to be done in any particular physical place. Giving employees some leeway on when and where they work will not only attract candidates (make sure you put it in the job ad), but it will also help you retain employees. Employees who enjoy flexible work hours will be very reluctant to give up this benefit by moving to a new employer.

What makes employees happy?

For your interest, here are some of the leading determinants of workplace happiness. Be sure to highlight them on your job advertisement where applicable when the time comes, while bearing in mind the demographic you are trying to attract.

7 Factors That Determine Workplace Happiness Levels[22]

1. Recognition
2. The right benefits
3. Interesting work
4. Healthy work-life balance
5. Growth potential and professional development
6. An inclusive, transparent and communicative environment
7. Autonomy

---

[22] https://gethppy.com/workplace-happiness/7-factors-determine-workplace-happiness-levels

CRAIG E BROWN

Role UVP Examples

iOS Developer

For our iOS Developer, our demographic will likely be younger educated people. We need to keep in mind what things are most likely to pique the interest of this demographic and attract them to this role. To keep things concise and Lean, we will use a few bullet points.

- Work on exciting projects for clients in variety of industries – never boring
- Amazing office – pool table, free lunch, dogs
- Flexible working

The first bullet point appeals to the candidate's desire to do important, exciting work, which can often be a challenge for employees to find in the earlier stages of their careers.

The second point will normally attract younger candidates.

The third point about flexible work hours will normally serve to both attract and retain employees. They get used to the lifestyle that comes with flexible working.

Inside Sales Representative

Our Inside Sales Representative is likely to be early to mid-career. They may have a family, but maybe not. This role is generally evenly split between the genders so we need a fairly broad range of incentives to attract candidates and retain them.

• Inbound-only role to convert missed leads
• Remote working
• Standard benefits – medical dental, paid vacation days

Our first bullet point quickly highlights that this is an inbound-role, meaning that they don't have to do any cold calling. You can think of this as a benefit because most Inside Sales Representative roles have an outbound component. It also demonstrates that this company has more leads than it can handle, illustrating that any decent Inside Sales Representative will be able to easily meet their quota.

Remote working is often offered with this type of role. As long as the employee has a few years of work experience and is able to manage their own time, there is no reason why they cannot work remotely. Software demos are all done online anyway. Smaller sales can be closed at a distance without ever needing to meet the client.

As this employee is likely to be mid-career, the standard benefits such as medical, dental and adequate holidays will be appealing.

Administrative Assistant

So, our Administrative Assistant will realistically be a woman. Rightly or wrongly, 96% of people in administrative roles in the US are women.[23] As a result, we need to create a role that will be most appealing and beneficial to women, mainly under the age of 45.

- Critical support of the CEO
- 4 hours per day - convenient schedule
- Local - easy to get to

The first point, which we will elaborate on later, demonstrates the importance of the role. This employee will allow the CEO to get her work done and keep the company moving.

From there, we really want to emphasize the convenience of the role and its ability to fit within an already busy schedule. If the employee is a parent, four hours is a window that can easily fit within a child's school schedule, which is very handy for parents. In addition, a short commute will be quite appealing to parents.

Your Canvas

Now I want to ask you to go back to your own Lean Recruiting Canvas and fill in Role UVP box. What's unique and interesting about the role itself? And what benefits can you offer that your competitors either are not offering or can't offer?

Bear in mind the demographics of your typical candidates. If you are looking to attract people outside of that demographic (for example more women, men, minorities, or veterans), think about what they will find compelling.

---

[23] https://www.huffingtonpost.com/2013/02/01/top-job-for-women-secretary-same-as-1950_n_2599560.html?guccounter=1

Sources: Where Will You Actually Find Candidates?

If you have been recruiting for any amount of time, you will already be aware of the main ways in which to source candidates: Boolean search, job ads, and agencies.

In this chapter, I will aim to increase your arsenal of sourcing methods and get you to think a little more creatively. More importantly, though, I want to ensure you are choosing the right method(s) that will help you find the best candidate as quickly as possible. That's what Lean is all about.

There are two main ways in which to find candidates, through active sourcing and through passive sourcing.

Active Sourcing versus Passive Sourcing

Active sourcing includes activities you conduct that are specific to the individual role at hand. If you are looking for an employee with a very specific skill set and a good education, chances are you will have to get out there and find them. Roles like Electrical Engineer, or Digital Marketing Manager are examples. If they are any good at what they do, they will not have to look for jobs. Jobs will find them. In this case, a 'post and pray' approach will not do the trick.

Active sourcing can also apply to roles like Administrative Assistant, just using slightly different tactics. It is unlikely that you will have to spend a lot of time searching for candidates. In this instance, the 'active bit' is your time spent crafting an appealing job advertisement that is targeted at the right type of applicant, ensuring that when people do apply, they are much more likely to be what you are looking for.

Active Sourcing generally includes methods like Boolean search (through job boards, internal databases and/or social media sites), job advertising, and making use of recruiting agencies. The information we fill in on our Lean Recruiting Canvas will largely be active sourcing methods.

Passive sourcing, on the other hand, will be more of a 'bait and set' strategy. You set up the infrastructure once, then wait to see what comes in over time. This method will ideally drive a pipeline of candidates to you, minimizing the amount of active searching that has to be done going forward. You would normally use this strategy when you are hiring a large number of people for the same role, such as a variety of management consultants for the Big Four accounting firms. They always need more good people.

Passive sourcing methods would include things like university outreach (such as participating in careers fairs and hosting hackathons), establishing a referral network internally, establishing and maintaining appropriate social media channels, and making sure you have a very candidate-friendly job site. While these channels are important, they will usually not be included on our Lean Recruiting Canvas as they are often not role-specific. That said, it is almost always a good idea to have passive sourcing in place. If you can get an easy win every now and again, why wouldn't you?

Active Sourcing

Boolean Search

The most obvious form of active sourcing is Boolean search. "Boolean search is a type of search allowing users to combine keywords with operators (or modifiers) such as AND, NOT and OR to further produce more relevant results."[24] For example, you might use the search string (Quota AND SaaS) when looking for software salespeople who sell Software-as-a-Service (SaaS) products.

It can be used with social media (mainly LinkedIn), job boards or even internal candidate databases. This type of technique is best used when the type of candidate is (a) hard to find and (b) ideally has searchable terms on their resume. You would normally use this for highly skilled people who are in the mid stages of their career. You need to know what you are looking for, how to create search strings, and how to avoid false positives. It takes a while to build up this skill, but it can be very worthwhile for the more challenging roles.

We could go into much more detail on how to conduct effective Boolean search, but, frankly, that would be a whole other book. There's lots of information online on how to build effective Boolean search strings. Once you know the basic operators and how they work, the rest is practice, including trial and error.

Job Advertising

Job ads could be seen as either an active or passive search strategy. But when done properly, in my opinion, it belongs in the active camp. If the job advertisement clearly outlines the Company USPs, the Role UVP and more salient points,

---

[24] https://www.webopedia.com/TERM/B/Boolean_search.html

you will have a fair-to-moderate chance at attracting the right person. But job ads that are not carefully written are a waste of time, both yours and the candidates'.

Using job ads is certainly no guarantee that you will attract the right person. However, it is a fairly simple exercise once you have all the right information at hand. And, you just might get lucky. If you post 20 job ads over the course of the year, and one of them attracts a really good hire without having to conduct an extensive search campaign, then it was worthwhile creating and posting the other 19.

The other positive outcome of creating a really good job advertisement is that it gives you something professional to link to when reaching out to candidates. Rather than just saying, "Hi Sandy, I have a really interesting inbound marketing role I would like to discuss with you," you can add, "Here is the link to the role." Having a job advertisement will help you come across as serious and   ready to hire as opposed to a recruiter who is looking for candidates to add to a database for future use.

Recruiting Agencies

This section, of course, is really more applicable to corporate recruiters. Agencies very rarely use other agencies.

While perceived as expensive, the use of external agencies can be very effective for finding really good candidates. When using agencies, I recommend you use no more than three for a role. More than that is hard to keep track of and you run the risk of having the same candidates submitted by more than one firm. Depending on the role, a good rule of thumb is to use one broad generalist, one specialist who focuses exclusively on the type of role you are placing, and another specialist who recruits a broad range of people for the type of industry you work in.

For example, if you are a financial services company in London looking for salespeople, use one broad generalist in London, use one agency that specializes in sales people, and another that focuses on recruitment for the financial services sector.

Here are a couple other tips when engaging the services of a recruiting agency:

1. Rather than focussing on their process, find out about their results.

Sure, you can find out about their process, but should you really care? This question is normally asked in order to gauge whether or not the agency will waste your time. But, if they are successful at finding talent for their clients the vast majority of the time, do you really want to go into the minutiae of how they did it?

A better use of your time would be to investigate if they have client testimonials on their LinkedIn profile. Other testimonials can be faked, but LinkedIn testimonials are more challenging to falsify. You could also ask them what their submission-to-hire ratio is for the type of role you are hiring for. If they don't know, this is a problem.

2. Don't quibble too much over rates.

If you want 'good,' pay for 'good.' If you beat agencies up too much on their rates, you will become a second-class client. You will generally only see the candidates that have been rejected by their other clients, who are paying the full fee. Think about your overall ROI – we'll get into this later in the Value Added chapter of this book.

Passive Sourcing

These methods may become part of your overall mix, but as previously discussed they won't likely make it onto the Canvas because they pertain to the company as a whole, rather than specific roles. The great thing about passive sources is that the infrastructure usually only has to be set up once and then can be used over and over again.

University Outreach

If large portions of your staff are expected to be recent graduates, then you will want to get on campus. There are a number of ways to do this.

The obvious one is having a presence at career fairs. This may be necessary, but there are more creative ways to be involved in campus life and get your brand out there.

In the tech space? Host a hackathon or sponsor a startup weekend. If you sponsor something, don't just erect a pull-up marketing banner in the corner of the room. Get t-shirts made and hand them out. If they are attractive and of good quality, your brand will be advertised all over campus for the rest of the year.

Looking for good marketing graduates? Assign all participants an individual UTM [25] and see who can drive the most qualified leads to your company. Pay them all for their efforts, say $200 per qualified lead. This will drive publicity throughout campus and will leave you with a solid shortlist of candidates come graduation time, not to mention a new customer or two.

---

[25] https://en.wikipedia.org/wiki/UTM_parameters

Basically, think about the types of candidates you need to hire (i.e. engineering, marketing, finance) and create events that cater to them, while at the same time providing your company with publicity and a pipeline of good graduate candidates.

Employee Referrals

This approach quite often gets overlooked, but if you run the numbers, it is usually very cost-effective. The idea here is that you offer a financial or other incentive to your current employees for referring candidates for your open positions. This is hands down the most effective way in most industries to get new employees who will actually perform well in the long run. Good employees tend to be attracted to others like themselves who have the same interests, skills and work ethic. Of course, you have to be ready to pay a cash reward directly to the referring employee. Some employees may be uncomfortable with this, so give them the option to have this reward donated to the charity of their choosing.

Normally, an employee referral fee will be between $1,000 and $5,000. You're probably thinking to yourself, "Gosh, that's pretty expensive."

It is, but you know what? It's cheaper than using recruiting agencies. It's also probably more cost-effective than having to wait three, four, five, six months to find someone to fill a role yourself. And it's certainly cheaper than having to let a poor performer go after only a few months. The only potential downside is that some feel that employee referrals may stifle diversity. While referrals are a great source of hires, you will need to monitor the diversity component.[26]

---

[26] https://www.nbcnews.com/business/consumer/why-job-referrals-can-hurt-company-s-diversity-n845106

Alerts

This is an extension of Boolean search. On most platforms where you can search for candidates, you can also set up alerts. Here's how it works.

1. You conduct a Boolean search for suitable candidates.
2. After time, your search becomes well honed and you find suitable candidates.
3. You opt in to Alerts, which will send you similar profiles as they come online, on a daily or weekly basis.
4. You check them as they come in and, over time, you harvest the best candidates. You can often even have these automatically added to your Applicant Tracking System.

Social Media

I suppose one could argue that not all companies need a social media presence, but it would be a pretty short debate. The key with social media is to determine which channels your target audience (in this case job candidates) spends their time, and then put your message in front of them.

If you don't have the time or the inclination to be constantly publishing content, then you should at least make sure things are tidied up. Make sure your LinkedIn company profile is concise and attractive. Make sure the company logo has been updated. Spend some time on it - you only have to do it once. Then do the same with Facebook, Twitter and whatever other social media channels you use. When a candidate does respond to an advertisement or a connection request from you, they will check you out online, and these things will help make the best possible impression.

Networking

Targeted networking can be valuable. Meetups can be a very effective way of locating talent over time, particularly in larger metropolitan areas where the groups can be quite granular. For the uninitiated, Meetup.com is a website that connects people with similar interests offline. It started off by connecting people with shared hobbies, but there is a now a significant business component as well.

If you are looking for iOS Developers in New York for example, consider joining the 'New York iOS Developer Meetup' group which has over 6,000 members. They regularly get over 100 attendees at their events.

Smaller cities have less niche-oriented groups, but they are still worth going to. When you go to these events, don't be shy. Tell people what you are after. Ask if they know anyone suitable. Be ready to hand out business cards.

Hybrid Sourcing™

The reason I focussed on passive sourcing previously is that some of them can be morphed into active sources if used properly. They are a hybrid of active and passive sourcing tactics called Hybrid Sourcing. And we can then use them on our Canvas. Here are a few ideas.

Reaching out to current employees via referral program

You have your referral program set up, which is a passive source of candidates. When you have a new role go live, send out an email to the appropriate team(s) informing them of the new opening and asking them to refer people. You'll likely be surprised at the positive response.

You will also wonder why they didn't tell you about these candidates earlier. It's because you hadn't asked. Any good marketer can tell you about the power of a Call-to-Action.[27] By overtly telling someone, "Email me today if you know someone who is interested in this role!" you are giving them permission to do something they had previously hesitated to do. It works.

Announcing new roles on social media

You should really do this as a matter of course. Whenever you have a new role posted, you should announce it on your social media platforms, along with a Call-to-Action - something like, "We are looking for a new part-time Administrative Assistant to support our CEO in a 12-month contract. Apply today or share with your network!"

You should also request that your employees share the posting with their networks as well for maximum exposure. Remember, you can only *request* this as employees are the owners of their social media profiles, but it can't hurt to ask.

Email past attendees of a hackathon or career fair

Remember all that stuff you did on campus? Keep the email addresses and participants when new roles come on board - remember to have an opt out clause for privacy in the email. Ask them to share with friends. Again, it is a simple win.

Deciding what methods to use

Really, what you want to think about with each of these channels is whether they are effective, and also time-effective. For example, posting a job advertisement for some roles isn't

---

[27] https://en.wikipedia.org/wiki/Call_to_action_(marketing)

really that effective but it also really won't take you a whole lot of effort or time to do it. Boolean Search, on the other hand, does take up a fair amount of time but sometimes it's the best way to find a really top candidate.

Methods will vary by role. As an example, the way you find an Administrative Assistant will be probably very different from how you find a Software Salesperson. Good software salespeople are generally hard to find because they're already working. You really have to get out there and find them rather than waiting for them to apply to a job ad.

This implies is that one of our main techniques is going to be implementing a robust and semantic Boolean word search campaign to get out there and find people who are not only qualified, but who we think would be a good fit for the role as well.

In contrast, I guarantee you that if you post a well written job advertisement for an Administrative Assistant, you will get 100 or 150 applications in a week. So posting is the best way to bring them in. The way that we derive value from posting is by later carefully assessing applicants, maybe even using automated assessments, to get those numbers down without eliminating the good candidates.

What we're really doing here is achieve the best results for the least amount of work, in keeping with our Lean principles.

A basic marketing tenet to bear in mind is to place your message where your customers (in this case, job candidates) are most likely to see it.

As an example, I came across an online recruiting agency a while back that only places people as staff for private yachts, globally. Their clients knew to go them because they knew their applicants would meet all basic criteria. Candidates knew to go to them there because they knew they would have access to the right kinds of jobs. If you are fortunate enough to own a large private yacht, then this is likely to be the best, and fastest, place to look for crew.

Sources Examples

iOS Developer

Let's get started determining Sources for our iOS role. We already know that finding top tech talent can be very difficult, sometimes exceedingly so. It will therefore require us to get creative in our search.

First of all, we will likely need to have a very precise and thorough Boolean search campaign. We will need to pick out the right keywords and execute the search with a great amount of effort, albeit a targeted effort.

The Boolean search is important, but we shouldn't ignore easier wins. We need to write a really effective job advertisement and announce the role using our various hybrid methods. Specifically, we will announce the job on our social media channels, making sure to link to the job advertisement and include a call-to-action.

Then, we will send out an email to our tech team encouraging them to let us know if they can think of anyone for the role.

Finally, we will email the participants of a hackathon we held a few months earlier to help spread the word.

Our bullet points for this box on our Canvass will look like this…

- Boolean search Indeed / LI
- Job Ad
- Hybrid announcements (social, referrals, hackathon)

Inside Sales Representative

For this role, we will also use a combination of methods at our disposal. Writing an effective job advertisement will be essential. Within sales, there can be overlapping meaning between various job titles, so being precise with the job description will be critical in attracting the right talent. For example, some ISR roles will require the employee to cold-call prospective leads. Other ISR roles won't have to do this because leads are instead the responsibility of a Sales Development Representative, or the inbound marketing team, or both.

A precise job advertisement will therefore allow candidates to filter themselves into the process, and where appropriate, filter themselves out of the process. The candidate will do the work for you.

Boolean search will also be an important part of this search. There should be lots of people online who have the requisite experience (at least on paper). Indeed.com has a nice function that tells us how recently someone updated their profile, a strong indicator that someone is actively searching for a new role. We can use this as a filter to get the numbers down.

And finally, we do not want to overlook our Hybrid reach-outs. As before, we will reach out to our employees to request referrals and also post on social media. We will also go back to contacts we made by attending the 'Sales and Marketing Innovators' Meetup in Boston.

Our bullets for this role will therefore be…

- Job Ad
- Boolean search – mainly Indeed.com
- Hybrid reach out – Meetup, referral, social media

Administrative Assistant

Realistically, a job advertisement is likely do the trick here. The key is to write a very accurate description of the role and what is expected. We will have a large pool of candidates to choose from. The key will be filtering down the numbers in a useful fashion, without eliminating the best candidate.

We will therefore have one bullet for this role…

- Job Advertisement

Your Canvas

Great, now please go ahead and fill in the Sources box of your Canvas for your role. Remember, this is a first go. If our assumptions - and therefore our methods - don't work, we can always adjust later.

Process: Create a Hiring Process for Each Role

Now that we have decided where we are most likely to find our candidates, we have to decide what steps we need to get to the best candidate, the purpose each step serves, and the ordering of the steps. We need to move quickly, as good talent doesn't wait around. Having a well-defined, agreed-upon process will enable us to do just that.

I cannot emphasize enough that it is absolutely critical to have a different process for each type of role.

A few years back, I worked with a tech firm in the San Francisco area. One of my first placements with them was for an enterprise level software sales executive who has had worked out very well for them. She had an endearing personality, which lined up well with the relationship-building role she was in.

We used a simple process that worked well for this hire. I sourced the candidates using various methods, and then had an initial screening call with each candidate to make sure they matched up with their resume (and to sell the role to them). I then handed the candidates over to the HR Manager, who quickly did her own screening call. Next, the candidates underwent a behavioral assessment to ensure their personality matched what was required for a consultative sales role, an important step for this kind of role. The final step involved a panel interview where the candidate was asked to demo a basic version of the employer's software solution to three members of the C-suite. It was a simple process and it worked well.

A few months later, I got back in touch to see if there were any other roles I could help with. I was put onto the CTO, Jim, who was looking for a fairly senior DevOps Software Engineer. I quizzed him in great depth about the role, including the hiring process. I specifically asked him what the interview process would look like after I hand a candidate over to him. He informed me that first he would do a phone call with each candidate, and then a behavioral assessment followed by a final interview. It was exactly the same process the company has used for the software sales executive.

"A behavioral assessment? Really?"

I asked Jim what the purpose of the behavioral assessment was. He paused for a minute, cleared his throat a little nervously, and informed me the CEO insisted on it for all hires. Jim went on to say he knew it wasn't an appropriate step for this type of role and was a little embarrassed by it. Of course, engineers need certain personal traits, but they are not the most important thing. It's more important that they know their field.

It then occurred to me to ask what happened if someone failed the assessment.

"We ignore the result," was his response. I was dumbfounded. So was he, but he was bound to the process. He had no say.

There are a few problems with this one-size fits all approach. Firstly, testing someone for something that isn't necessary for their role will make them wonder if you actually know what you're doing, so it doesn't build confidence.

Secondly, it is literally pointless. You don't get any useful information out of it.

And finally, it wastes time. In this case, it would have wasted at least three days by the time the test is sent out, completed by the candidate and the results analyzed. Remember, time is our enemy. As I have pointed out before, good talent moves on quickly. The candidate may very well be interviewing with two to three other employers at the same time. They may choose to not even complete your assessment, because it is cumbersome and unnecessary.

The Lean Recruiting Toolkit endorses role-specific hiring processes that change with each role. To be more precise, it also changes within each role over time because the Process is Agile and adapts to external and internal factors, aka Catalysts.

The reason for this is that each role, and its environment, is different. As a result, we need to prove different points for each role. For a sales role, we need to prove that our candidates have the right personality so a personality assessment could be appropriate. For an administrative role, we may need to prove that they can use Microsoft Excel so we could put them through an online test to evaluate their Excel skills.

Your recruitment process should only include the steps that are relevant to proving that the candidate can perform their role well. Nothing more, nothing less.

What do you need to prove?

For each role, we have points that need to be proven in order to hire someone. Most 'points' will come from the Ideal Employee box.

What are the most common steps and what are they used for?

So now we're going to have a quick look at some of the main steps that are often used in the hiring process. And as we get further into this discussion, we'll look at a couple of things you possibly haven't heard of before.

Screening Interview

The screening interview is included in most interview processes. Normally, it's a quick sanity check on the phone between you and the candidate, just to make sure there aren't any major discrepancies between what you've seen on paper and what you're hearing on the phone. You should do this step before you bring the candidate into the office for further interviews for most jobs, but not all.

The number one reason for conducting a screening call is to sell the candidate on the opportunity. The more they are sold on the opportunity, the more likely they will eagerly complete all of the remaining steps in the hiring process. They will be more likely to wait if there is a delay. And they will also be more likely to be patient for an offer, even if they already have one in hand from another employer.

Assessments

Assessments are the new kid on the recruiting block, particularly online assessments. You can do coding tests for software developers, video assessments, behavioral assessments when personality is really important, and proficiency tests with various software packages. These assessments are an important part of a recruiter's arsenal, but just remember that technology is there to complement a recruiter, not replace one. Use assessments when they are appropriate. Leave them out when they are not.

Main / Final Interview

The main interview - there's almost always one - could be a panel interview, a role play, a presentation, or a practical exercise. As a main interview, you could give someone a two-week trial to see how they make out, or you could use a combination of approaches. The point is to make sure there is actually a reason for having this step. Sometimes there isn't. This is the part of the Process that often has an ill-defined purpose and an insufficiently tight structure.

Checks

Checks are very important. You will should always do reference checks as a matter of course, but remember, no one ever has a bad reference. You often have to read between the lines. One of the best probing questions I have come across when speaking with a reference is "What advice would you give me to ensure I get the best performance possible from Sam?" They are generally not expecting the question. Also, it implies that the candidate is going to get the job, which means you're likely get a very honest answer.

Salary checks also are important for sales roles because if someone has beaten their quota, then they should be earning their entire potential bonus. A good way to check performance is to ask for proof of earnings.

What order should my steps be in?

As a rule of thumb, you should attempt to prove the easiest things first. In low volume roles where there the emphasis is on Boolean search, you will be discounting candidates who don't meet basic criteria. For example, you may wish to discount Software Developers without a degree in Computer Science. This can easily be seen on the resume.

For high volume candidates, it may be more appropriate to put candidates through some sort of screening process toward the beginning to eliminate people who don't pay attention to detail. You should be aiming to retain the highest number of candidates with positive results before you have your colleagues participate in time-intensive interviews. Aim to do this without eliminating any good candidates.

As a general rule, you should alternate human and technological contact to keep candidates on board. If you do two automated assessments in a row, you will lose a lot of good candidates. They want to know that a human being is on the other end of the assessment.

Keep the number of steps to an absolute minimum. Once you have proven your points, stop. Then hire someone. Don't fall into the trap of a final panel interview with no structure or purpose to it, or other unnecessary steps.

And finally, define success for each step, and then automat progression to next step rapidly. When one step is complete, you should know exactly to do next and in what time frame.

.

Process Examples

Time to now work through a couple of Process examples. I've given you some ideas above, but sometimes it's best just to see how things work in practice.

iOS Developer

Let's have a look at what we need to 'prove' in order to hire our iOS Developer. Below are the points from our 'Ideal Employee' box.

- Bachelor's Degree in Computer Science or Electrical Engineering
- Great knowledge of Swift programming language
- Object-oriented programming experience
- Multiple published iOS apps

For the first point, it's easy to assess education from a resume. It needs to be proven later, of course, but for the time being, if it is on the resume, assume it is the truth.

In points two and three, you're looking for someone who can code very well and quickly, specifically in the Swift coding language. The candidate also has to have a good working knowledge of object-oriented programming.

You should be able to find these terms on a resume. Only speak with candidates who have both of these terms written on their resumes. I would advise against actually searching for the term 'iOS Developer' because the candidate may be using something different like 'App Developer' or 'Mobile Developer.' If you can believe it, I once saw an iOS Developer use 'Change Agent of the Future' as his job title. It takes all kinds.

If you search for the coding language and other relevant hard skills, you will have more success finding appropriate technical candidates.

After a brief screening call to let them know there is actually a human being on the other end of this process (and also as a quick sanity check), we should give them a remote coding test. If they pass that, then we would invite them in for a panel interview, where our technical team can discuss the coding test results and probe more deeply. One of the reasons for doing this is to make sure that the candidate was actually the person who did the coding test, in order to prevent fraudulent results - it happens. Assume they cheated. Hope for the best, but plan for the worst.

I had a client in Boston who once found that some candidates were having overseas coders take coding tests for them. They would only find out about the fraud once the person was in the job and couldn't code to save their lives. One guy admitted he cheated, and the process changed.

On the fourth point, anyone who has published apps, and is proud of their work, will link them right into their resumes.

Easy enough.

So here is our process…

1. Source candidates.
2. Screen for 'Swift', 'Object-oriented' and links to published apps.
3. Conduct a screening call to sell opportunity and make them feel the love.
4. Email them the link for the coding test. In the same email, outline entire recruiting process from start to finish to help them follow along.
5. If they pass coding test, conduct a panel interview to verify coding test results and assess motivation and general fit with the team.
6. Make the offer.
7. Do checks to verify education and employment history.
8. Have them sign the contract.

Inside Sales Representative

Like our previous example, we'll start by working out what needs to be proven. What makes an Ideal Employee for this role? Here are the points from our Ideal Employee box:

- Two-year minimum track record of exceeding quota selling SaaS software solutions
- Experience conducting online, remote demos
- Team player - check modesty

First of all, we are looking for someone with a two-year track record in software sales. We have decided that this is adequate enough experience for our purposes. We have hired other people with that amount of experience and they have worked out. So, initially, we can check this using the resume.

We can then prove it later by getting reference from employers to confirm the length of their tenure. We can also ask for copies of their W2s for the last two years[28] to verify total earnings. By verifying total earnings, we will prove beyond a shadow of a doubt that our candidate has met their sales quota. How? For sales people, income is broken into two main parts: base salary and bonus. They only receive their whole bonus if they meet or beat quota. If total earnings exceed the base salary plus anticipated bonus, they have sold what they were expected to sell[29] . Simple.

With regards to conducting online demos, this can usually be found on the resume. Some people do leave it off. You can verify it initially during a screening call. You can always get the candidate to present something remotely as part of the interviewing process. I am a big fan of asking the candidate to present the very solution they will be selling on the job. If it is a very complicated solution, you can have them present a pared down version to keep things straightforward.

Here, we are checking their comfort with technology, persuasion skills, and ability to learn quickly. Remember, they will not be perfect in this first presentation. How could they be? - you haven't trained them yet.

And for the final point, we are checking for modesty. It is a very strong indicator that someone is a team player[30], which is extremely important for consultative technical sales. In fact, when the employee is permitted to work remotely, this has to be an extra strong trait to compensate for the fact that the employee will rarely, if ever, be in the same room as coworkers.

---

[28] For Canadian readers, the American W2 is the equivalent to the T4. For British and Irish readers, this is the P60.

[29] It is perfectly legal to ask candidates for proof of earnings in most jurisdictions, but not all. Check before you ask the candidate.

[30] https://hbr.org/2011/06/the-seven-personality-traits-o

I know, you will check for this trait during the interview. You are a very good judge of character so it won't be a problem for you.

Wrong. Use a behavioral assessment.

There may have been issues years ago with the accuracy of behavioral assessments, but this is no longer the case. The keys to getting good results from behavioral assessments are (a) trust the criteria set by the experts and (b) then trust the results.

Don't change the criteria because you think you are smarter than the behavioral scientists who developed the test. You aren't and neither am I. Also, discipline yourself to trust the results, either positive or negative. One way to do this is to set these assessments early in the process, before you form your own opinion of the candidate.

Based on all of the above, here is the Process we'll use...

1. Source candidates.
2. Conduct a screening call to check basic match.
3. Send link to behavioral assessment. In the same email, provide entire recruiting process to instill confidence and keep them on board throughout the duration.
4. Conduct a panel interview to go over their resume and conduct remote role play presenting employer's solution.
5. Make an offer.
6. Do checks. W2 to confirm earnings, and therefore quota track record. Also check references from previous employer.
7. Have them sign the contract.

Administrative Assistant

Again, let's first of all think about what information we need. What do we need to prove? Below are our Ideal Employee points.

- Type 50 words per minute error free
- Strong ability to use Microsoft Word, Outlook, PowerPoint and Excel
- Ability to prioritize multiple tasks and work to deadline where appropriate

So this type of role is different to the other two in that you don't really have to search for candidates. If you post the job ad, you will get lots of applicants, especially if you have a well written ad. The task really is about getting the numbers down without accidentally eliminating the best candidate.

Realistically, our first step will be to advertise the job. But we need to get our numbers down in a way that will keep our ideal candidate in the running. I have seen a few creative ways to do this.

The first way would be to instruct the candidate to complete a behavioral assessment for outward facing roles. Maybe you have decided that personality will be a key determinant of who gets this job. Only candidates who complete and pass the assessment should move on to the next stage.

But let's say for our purposes other skills are more important, like attention to detail. After all, who wants to hire an administrator who misses the finer points under pressure? One of our key points is the ability to multitask, which means they can pay attention to a whole bunch of unrelated details.

So here's an idea. I have seen it done a few times and think it is a very elegant solution. At the very *end* of your job ad, write something like this...

"When you apply, please include the word 'Elephant' in the subject line of your application. As you can imagine, we get lots of applicants, but we are only interested in candidates who pay attention to the finer details. This will also let us know you have read the entire job description."

A lot of people will apply for administrator roles without having read the description. They may even apply on a smartphone. They just think to themselves, "Oh, I can do that." Then click 'Submit'. Now it's on your desk to sift through. They haven't a clue if they are qualified for the role, or if they are even interested in it.

This 'Elephant' clause, which is positioned at the very bottom of the job ad, should eliminate up to 90% of candidates - the ones that don't pay attention to detail.

After that, we can do a quick screening call to verify our other points about typing and the Microsoft Office Suite, and, of course, to sell the opportunity.

Finally, they should come in for an interview, largely consisting of a typing test and a proficiency test in the relevant Microsoft Office products. Don't do this remotely, as again, this is open to fraud. Have them do it in the office under a bit of pressure - another way to assess multitasking ability.

As another quick tip, let them know in advance that you are going to be testing these skills in the office. Some will cancel because they have falsified claims on their resumes, so this will save you time.

So, here is our Process...

1. Advertise job, including simple task.
2. Do screening call.
3. Conduct office interview - including typing and Office proficiency tests.
4. Make an offer.
5. Check references.
6. Have them sign the contract.

Your Canvas

One final note. We are only looking for the must-haves in the above process. If you are lucky enough to have a number of candidates who meet these criteria - great. You can then choose the person who is most likely to get along with the grumpy janitor. But verify the essential criteria first. You won't regret it in the long run.

Please go ahead and fill in the Process section of your own Canvas.

CRAIG E BROWN

Key Metrics: Ratio Analysis to Measure Progress

In this chapter, we're going to have a look at Key Metrics. The point of doing so is for you to be able to measure your own performance going forward and make adjustments to your Process as necessary. If you can't measure it, you can't fix it.

What are Key Metrics?

Key Metrics are factors that you measure to make sure that your strategy and related assumptions are robust. This is where we start laying the foundation for the Kaizen model of continuous improvement.

That way, if something does go wrong during our hiring process, we can solve it much more quickly than we would be able to normally, without wasting time or money.

Once you set your metrics, visit them about once a week. Key Metrics are one source of Latent Catalysts™, which we discuss later in the book. I would even go so far as to put a little reminder in your calendar to visit the metrics and do the numbers. Honestly, it'll take you only a little time each week and then you can do a quick evaluation and see how you're doing. If a Catalyst comes up, or if there is a change in requirements or the job, or something's not quite working out, then you can revisit the entire Canvas.

Time-to-Hire

One major Key Metric that is quite often used is Time-to-Hire. This means measuring the time from when you start step one of your process (usually posting the job) until you actually hire someone. This measurement may be good on the macro scale for measuring long term progress within a company, but it's not quite granular enough for our needs during individual recruitment requisitions. If something goes wrong during the recruitment process, or just needs adjusting, we won't know which part of our process needs tweaking with this sort of metric.

The other issue with measuring Time-to-Hire is that it creates time-pressure on the recruiter to hire the first applicant who meets criteria, rather than necessarily the best applicant.

Ratio Analysis

We're going to use Ratio Analysis as our key measurement tool. This means examining the number of candidates who advance from one step to the next in our hiring process. Using these measurements, we can do analysis. If the ratios are consistently 2:1 between most steps, but 7:1 between one particular step and the next, then we will know to look more closely at that specific step to identify the issue.

The best way to understand ratio analysis is to use a specific example. Let's go back to Administrative Assistant role and revisit the process.

The first ratio to analyze is the advance from Step 1 (Advertise job, including simple task) to Step 2 (Do screening

THE LEAN RECRUITING TOOLKIT

call). Out of all the people who applied and remembered to put the word 'Elephant' in the subject line, how many did I actually invite to do a screening call?

We don't really want to go back in the recruiting process any earlier than this because we're anticipating a very high number of applicants for this role, even with the subject line qualifier in place. For our example, let's say the ratio is 15:1.

It may turn out that you think this ratio is reasonable. Or, you might look at the ratio and think, "15-to-1? I thought I did a good job at selling the role and explaining it properly in the job ad. Why is that ratio not lower?"

If you are unhappy with your ratio, then you can go back and analyze your job description in greater detail. You may want to have someone from your marketing department to look at it - they will likely have copywriting experience, which is always helpful for job ads.

Your conversation could be very telling. You may have included too much detail on the day-to-day activities making it appear overwhelming. Or, it could be the inverse. Perhaps your job description is so spartan that candidates are not able to determine if it is something they want to apply for. Or, maybe it's that you left out a key component, like proficiency at Microsoft Excel. In this case, you simply adjust the advert, re-advertise, and continue to monitor your ratio. If any of these are the case then you can revise the advertisement based on the feedback and you are back in business. If the ratio worsens after you make the changes, go either back to the original version, or make a different change. Simple.

The great thing about making and monitoring your change, once it is refined, is that you can back re-use the process the next time you are sourcing for the same type of role. You

181

keep your completed Canvas and pull just it out of the drawer when you need it.

Let's now analyze the progression from Step 3 (Conduct office interview - including typing and Office proficiency test) to Step 4 (Make an offer). Out of the candidates that actually complete a full interview how many of them were made an offer? If your ratio is too high, you go to the Hiring Manager, or whoever else is involved, and ask for their opinion. It might be something as simple as you have been sending the Hiring Manager too many candidates in too short a time and they are becoming paralysed with indecision. It can really be as simple as that.

It could also be that you've just unfortunately brought the wrong candidates forward. Maybe some of the traits they have, or some of the information on the resume wasn't quite what the interview panel was looking for. Again, you might have to do a bit of readjustment on your part. Perhaps you find out that the interview panel didn't clearly express to you that the candidate has to have experience putting together simple financial reports on a weekly basis as part of their job. If this is the case, you need to go back, adjust your Canvas and your job ad, and get more candidates in. Then continue to monitor your own progress.

Ratio analysis can easily be used between your steps to see how many people are progressing, in order to identify whether or not there may be an issue, but figuring how to solve the issue will be up to you.

Ratio analysis will work differently for each role depending on what your Process is. If you use an Applicant Tracking System (ATS), there's often a function that tracks recruitment performance. Set it up, track it, and run a report outlining your performance.

If you work in a smaller organization, you can really just use a simple spreadsheet to track your ratios. All you have to do is enter your candidate names in Column 1. Column 2 can be the date for the screening call, Column 3 can be the panel interview etc. Every time a candidate is scheduled to complete the next step, write the date in the appropriate cell. When you want to analyze your ratios, assuming the numbers are manageable, you just add them up.

Key Metrics Examples

OK, let's give you a few examples that you can sink your teeth into.

iOS Developer

Let's begin with our iOS Developer position and examine what Key Metrics we need to look at, and what they will tell us. In this example, we're going to skip the very first possible ratio where we would track Step 1 (Source candidates) to Step 2 (Screen for 'Swift', 'Object-oriented' and links to published apps). The reason for this is that is Step 2 is effectively accomplished as we are searching through resumes. We would be screening for 'Swift' and 'Object-Oriented' as we source.

So the first ratio we will be tracking is the progression from Step 2 (Conduct a screening call) to Step 3 (Email them the link for the coding test).

The screening call is to make sure that the candidate's type of experience and the length of their experience matches up with what's on the resume. If you find a problematic ratio here, you need to dig deeper into the process. The main reason someone may not advance from the screening call to the coding test is that they have the right keywords on their resume but have embellished their experience too much. In other words, they have an 'aspirational' resume.

Another reason could be that they have the right kind of experience but not the right length of experience - perhaps the dates are a little vague on their resume. If this ratio begins to balloon, you may want to revisit the key words you are looking for, or perhaps the emphasis you are giving each of them.

The next metric we'll look at is the progression from Step 4 (Email them the link for the coding test) to Step 5 (Conduct a panel interview). This is basically a pass / fail coding test. If your ratio gets too high here (too many people are failing the test), there may be a few possible explanations. Firstly, there may just not be enough talent locally whose technical abilities are up to scratch. They try the test but just cannot pass. I have also seen an example where a coding test was created by a technical person internally which is biased toward their own skillset. It would be exceedingly difficult to find a perfect match in this instance. Finally, some coding tests unnecessarily screen out people who are more-or-less fluent in English, but perhaps are not native speakers. If you need native speakers, then this is fine. If you are more interested in their coding ability, then this high benchmark may be overly restrictive.

The next ratio we'll look at is Step 5 (Conduct a panel interview) to Step 6 (Make an offer). If we find an odd issue here, we'll need to assess the panel interview.

We're first going to discuss the results of the coding test in the panel interview itself for a couple of reasons. It will give us the opportunity to go into much more depth on the candidate's coding experience. It allows us to check their creativity and whether or not they can work independently.

But most importantly, we get to make sure that the online coding test wasn't a fraudulent submission. As indicated previously, sometimes candidates will hire coders to complete coding tests on their behalf, and we want to make sure that's not the case.

Our next metric will be Offer to Checks. This is the first step where the ball is in the candidate's court. Sometimes they will reject an offer, and we don't get to the stage where we make a check. One of the main reasons for that is they've started receiving offers from other companies, and they feel they're in the position to negotiate a bit more, or sometimes they just walk away completely, because they've taken an offer from another employer. In either case, one of the things you'd really want to examine is how quickly your recruiting process is moving along. If it's taking too long to get to this step, then you will lose candidates. You may need to make an adjustment to get you to the finish line faster.

Our final metric will be examining our Checks to Contract ratio. Here, we're looking at seeing whether or not people pass reference checks, and whether or not their university degree stands up. Sometimes people do falsify university degrees, and you may be thinking to yourself, "Well, this person's gotten this far, and they certainly know their coding, it's just the degree that's holding them back."

True, but what you have now is a candidate who has already misled you once, and they haven't even gotten the job yet, so you may want to think about whether or not that is somebody you really want to advance with. On the flipside, you may wish to adjust your requirements so that the candidates do not need a university degree. If this coder is good enough without one, maybe there are others out there like her.

With employment reference checks, in my experience, there are no bad ones.

Candidates only put forward referees that they know are going to give them a glowing review, so really you want to examine things like what position did the reference hold? Was it just a friend of the candidate's who worked in the company at the same level, or was it their direct supervisor, and what sort of things are they saying about them?

So, to summarize, here is what we will put in our Key Metrics box on our Canvas.

1. Screening call to Coding Test
2. Coding Test to Panel Interview
3. Panel Interview to Offer
4. Offer to Checks
5. Check to Contract

Inside Sales Representative

Now we'll move onto our Inside Sales Representative role. Again, we're going to skip the Sourcing to Screening Call ratio, and we'll move onto the Screening Call to Behavioral Assessment ratio. Similar to our last role, really the main reasons for not moving someone forward from a screening call to the next step would be that their resume is a bit misleading; they've got the right keywords, but not enough experience, for example.

Our next ratio will be Behavioral Assessment to Panel Interview. This is another example of a pass/fail situation. Did they pass the behavioral assessment or did they fail it? This does require a bit of self-discipline, because you might think, "This person's good on paper. I had my screening call with them, they sounded really good."

Really, the key here is to be very strict with yourself, and do not override the results of the behavioral assessment. It is sometimes very hard to do, but it is a 'must', especially for employers who want to eliminate unconscious bias. Candidates in this instance are assessed 100% objectively. Inversely, if you weren't particularly keen on someone, but they get a glowing behavioral assessment, then you must discipline yourself to push them forward to the next stage, regardless of what your personal opinion is of the person.

Our next ratio will be Panel Interview to Offer. In this panel interview we're doing a remote role play. Some of things that the interview panel will be assessing are the candidate's ability to handle technology and the ability to conduct remote software demos. They'll be looking to see what the candidate's persuasion skills are, and what their knowledge of formal sale processes are like (Sandler , Challenger , SPIN). They'll be looking to see how much homework the candidate did on the actual software solution itself. If they pass this phase, then they move onto the offer.

The next ratio of course will be Offer to Checks. This will, as in previous examples, be largely an indicator as to whether our Process is fast enough. If the candidates are abandoning us at this stage for other employment offers, our process is too slow, or the offer not compelling enough.

Finally, we move onto the last ratio, which is Checks to Contract. So again we're checking references like we did in the last role, but here we're also checking income (so long as it is legal to do so in the jurisdiction you find yourself.) If someone's total income is greater than their On-Target-Earnings (OTE)[31], then they have been honest about their

---

[31] OTE is the total pay a salesperson receives if they exactly meet their quota. It is base salary plus commissions.

sales prowess. They have beaten their quotas as they have indicated.

So, in our Key Metrics box, we will use the following steps on our Canvas…

1. Screening Call to Behavioral Assessment
2. Behavioral Assessment to Panel Interview
3. Panel Interview to Offer
4. Offer to Checks
5. Checks to Contract

Administrative Assistant

Finally, we'll move onto our Administrative Assistant role. We did examine this briefly early in the chapter, but we'll look at all the ratios now. The first ratio that we'll look at is our Job Application to Screening Call. As you remember, we put a very simple task at the bottom of the job advertisement where we ask all job applicants to use the word 'Elephant' in the subject line of their job applications. That's a great way to ensure that they have read the entire job ad.

Once we actually get those applications in, it's at this stage we will go through those resumes and look for keywords and relevant experience. How many of them meet the requisite experience (at least on paper) that we have advertised on the job ad? If they have the experience, they advance to the screening call. If they don't, they're rejected by email.

Our next ratio will be Screening Call to Office Interview. During our screening call, we're double-checking to make sure that the person does actually have the type of experience we're looking for and the depth of experience as well. If they do, they move onto the next stage. If they don't, they're rejected.

Our next ratio is Office Interview to Offer. The office interview will have a panel interview, but the candidate is also going to be doing a couple of tests onsite. They'll be doing a typing test to make sure that they can indeed type 50 words-per-minute error-free, and they will also do a Microsoft Office test where they'll be tested on Word, PowerPoint, Excel, and Outlook. If they pass all of those things, and also the panel interview, then they move onto the offer stage.

Offer to References will be next. I would suspect for this type of role, that's going to be a very low ratio. When most people receive an offer for this type of role, they are generally very happy to accept it as there are tons and tons of applicants to compete with.

The next ratio of course is References to Contract. Again, this involves going back and speaking to the references that have been provided. Once again, there are no bad references, so you need to not only examine the relationship between the candidate and the referee, but also dive a lot deeper into the type of experience they had, and how good they actually were at their last role.

Here are our bullets for the Key Metrics for this role on our Canvas...

1. Job Application to Screening Call
2. Screening Call to Office Interview
3. Office Interview to Offer
4. Offer to References
5. References to Contract

Your Canvas

Now, go back to your own Canvas and fill in this section. You want to focus on what your Process is and what the most important parts are for you to track. See you in the next chapter.

Cost Structure: What is the Total Cost of Hiring?

In this chapter, we are going to examine our Cost Structure, and then we'll conclude the Lean Recruiting Canvas by examining the Value Added. The two of them are joined at the hip, as together, they are what we need to determine the Return-on-Investment (ROI) of hiring our employee.

In the earlier chapters, specifically the Problem and Solution chapters, we were bridging the recruiting function with the needs of the company as a whole. In subsequent sections, we internalized the requisition into the recruiting department to make a plan of action.

Now that our initial plan is complete, we need to bring everything back to the business and justify the new hire in financial terms.

I know that you are in recruiting and the budget doesn't always fall under your remit. Why are we examining this? Well, recruiting is part of the overall business, and really, we want to show our external partners within the company that we've given a fair amount of thought to whether or not it actually makes sense for the company to hire someone. By committing some time and thought, we can take our plan to the rest of the business and say, "Look, this is what I've come up with. Here are the numbers that prove this makes sense. What do you think?" This approach provides further evidence that we are following the right course of action and helps secure buy-in from the business.

And, of course, if the numbers don't stack up, you will also have the opportunity to just pull the plug on the hire or make adjustments to your plan before you charge ahead.

Before we get into the numbers, let me give you a working definition of what the Cost Structure is.

The Cost Structure is the annualized cost of recruiting and employing a new employee.

Cost Structure includes initial recruiting costs as well as the cost of employing someone on an ongoing basis, plus any other related costs you can think of (training, onboarding etc.). We're going to add all this up and come up with an annual figure.

Let's have a quick look at how the numbers work. If you are not a big fan of math, you can download a spreadsheet that will do the calculations for you by visiting the following link...

http://calculator.JustInTimeRecruiting.com

Here is a basic formula you can use:

HR Professional Costs
+
One-off Advertising Costs
+
Software Costs
+
Recruiting Agency Costs
+
Other One-off Costs
=
Sub-total

÷

Average Length of Tenure

=
Sub-total

+
Annual Cost of Employee

=

Cost Structure

Let's now go back and break these down step by step.

HR Professional Costs

The formula for calculating the HR Professional Costs related to the recruitment process is:

Daily rate of HR Professional[32] × # days spent working on requisition

The Daily Rate of the HR Professional can be calculated using this:

Annual salary X 1.5 / 225 days per year

Let's delve into this further.

So first we have to take into account the recruiter's annual salary (i.e. your annual salary) The reason for this is that your salary is part of your employer's cost of recruiting, and you have to spend time recruiting this new employee. You could be going through hundreds of resumes and multiple interviews after all.

We're going to take the dollar costs of your salary and multiply it by 1.5. Your employer incurs costs over and above your salary to employ you that are shared among all employees (such as utilities, heat, power, rent), plus pension contributions for you. These extra costs normally add up to about 50% on top of your basic salary, and sometimes more.

Then, we take that number and divide it by 225, which is approximately the number of working days in one year. There

---

[32] This is the person who actually does the recruiting work internally, fills out and executes the Lean Recruiting Canvas.

are of course, 365 days in a year, but we need to subtract the weekend days, paid vacation days, national holidays, the odd sick day, and a few other things. The true number can be anywhere from 200 to 240, depending on how senior you are in your career and what country you live in. You can plug in a different number if you like, but 225 is a good average. This will give us the cost that your employer incurs employing you for one day.

We are then simply going to multiply that daily cost by the number of days we think it's going to take you to work on this requisition and fill the position. Now, we're going to have to be a little bit creative here, because realistically, most people don't sit down at 9am in the morning, work on one requisition all day, go home, and back the next day to start up again. The realty is, recruitment is done in bits and pieces, so think about how many hours you put into it and try to come up with an estimate on how many days that's going to take you. This will give you a total initial cost for your work on this requisition.

Advertising and Software Costs

We also have to think about advertising costs and other software costs. How much does it cost you to put up the job advertisement on a niche website? Are there other software costs? Maybe you're using a behavioral assessment tool, and you have to think about how much that costs. Add those in as one-off advertising and software costs.

Recruiting Agency Costs

How much will it cost you to make use of the services of a recruiting agency? This point is obviously only applicable to corporate recruiters. Recruiting agencies are not cheap, so you have to factor that in as well.

Next Steps

We're going to add all these costs up, including any other one-off costs associated with the hire, and then we're going to divide by the Average Length of Tenure in years, to give you an annualized figure of your initial costs. If the average employee at your company works for three years, you take the total annual figure and divide by three.

Annual Cost of Employee

Use the same calculation we did for your own annual cost (i.e. in the HR Professional Costs section above) to calculate the Annual Cost of Employee, plus any expected bonus:

Annual Cost of Employee = (Employee Salary × 1.5) + Bonus

To break this down further, we are calculating the costs associated with employing the new employee (i.e. salary and associated costs plus any bonuses). To do this, we take the employee's annual salary figure and multiply it by 1.5 to take into account associated costs of employing someone just like you did for your own salary. Then we add in any annual bonus they may receive to give us an Annual Cost of Employee figure.

The Final Calculation

To calculate our final total for the overall Cost Structure, add the Annual Cost of Employee to everything else we have previously calculated.

You will note, perhaps somewhat surprisingly, that all of the one-off costs, particularly when they are averaged out over the average tenure of an employee, really don't add up to much in the grand scheme of things.

Our main expense (or investment depending on how you look at it) is the salary of the employee.

CRAIG E BROWN

Cost Structure Examples

Now let's have a look at how the numbers pan out with our three examples.

iOS Developer

HR Professional Costs = (Daily Rate of HR Professional = (Annual salary × 1.5 / 225 days per year)) × # days working on requisition = $800
+
One-off advertising costs = $150
+
Software costs = $100
+
Recruiting Agency Costs = $0
+
Other One-off Costs =$0
=
Sub-total = $1,050
÷
Average Length of Tenure = 2.3 years
=
Sub-total = $456.52
+

Annual Cost of Employee = ((Salary × 1.5) + Bonus) = $67,500
=
$67,956.52

Cost Structure = $67,956.52

So to begin with, our HR Professional costs are $800. This is an annual salary of $40,000 × 1.5 to give the real costs of employing you. Then we divide by 225 to give a day rate. Finally we multiply by 3 days as we estimate it will take a total of 24 hours (3 working days) to do all of the work in hiring for this role.

We then estimate that we will spend $150 on advertising the role. We will also spend $100 on a coding assessment tool. In this case, we will not use a recruiting agency. There are no other one-off costs.

If we do a quick subtotal, we get $1,050.

We then divide by our average length of tenure to get an annualized figure for these costs, which we find out from our CRM is 2.3 years, giving us an annualized figure of $456.52.

Then we add this number to the annual salary of the employee, again times 1.5. The salary is $45,000, so this is $67,500. There is no bonus.

The total figure for our Cost Structure is $67,956.52.

While it will be impossible to give us a 100% accurate figure here, it is really interesting to see that the bulk of the costs are the employee's salary and associated costs.

Inside Sales Representative

HR Professional Costs = (Daily Rate of HR Professional = (Annual salary × 1.5 / 225 days per year)) × # days working on requisition = $500
+
One-off Advertising Costs = $0
+
Software Costs = $110
+
Recruiting Agency Costs = $0
+
Other One-off Costs = $0
=
Sub-total = $610
÷
Average Length of Tenure = 3 years
=
Sub-total = $203.33
+
Annual Cost of Employee = ((Salary × 1.5) + Bonus) = $90,000
=

$90,203.33

Cost Structure = $90,203.33

In this case, our HR Professional accounts for $500 in costs. This is a salary of $50,000 × 1.5. We then divide by 225 days, and then multiple by 1.5 working days (12 hours) working on the role.

We post the job on a free job board so will have no advertising costs. The job board we are using, however, charges us for every time we reach out to a candidate, in this case a fee of $2. We estimate we will have to reach out to 30 candidates, so our software costs will be $60 here. In addition, we want our candidate to sit a behavioral assessment, but we pay a small monthly fee for this. We will attribute $50 to this, for a total of $110 in software costs.

Our plan is not to use a recruiting agency for this role, so that cost is $0. There are no other costs that we can think of, so our subtotal is $610. The average length of tenure for these types of roles we estimate to be 3 years, so this figure annualized is $203.33, which is quite reasonable.

Our Inside Sales Representative has a base salary of $40,000, so if we multiply this by 1.5, we get $60,000. They will also have a bonus of $30,000 if they hit their targets, so the Total annual cost for the employee of $90,000.

If we add our one-off costs to this, we get $90,203.33. Again, the majority of costs are associated with salary.

Administrative Assistant

HR Professional Costs = (Daily Rate of HR Professional = (Annual salary × 1.5 / 225 days per year)) × # days working on requisition= $160
+
One-off Advertising Costs = $0
+
Software Costs = $50
+
Recruiting Agency Costs = $0
+
Other One-off Costs = $0
=
Sub-total = $210
÷

Average Length of Tenure = 1 year

=

Sub-total = $210

+

Annual Cost of Employee = ((Salary × 1.5) + Bonus) = $20,250

=

$20,460

Cost Structure = $20,460

Here, we will assume our HR Professional has an annual salary of $32,000 and only spends 6 hours total working on this role. That would be 0.75 days. If we do the math, this gives us a total of $160.

We will assume that we are using a free advertising tool, but that we will be using and paying for the assessments they will be doing when they come in for the office interview. Let's attribute $50 to this. Our initial subtotal will be $210.

Since this is a one-year contract, any one-off costs incurred are already annualized. We will therefore make this '1 year'.

The salary of our new employee is $13,500 (remember, she is working 20 hours per week) with no bonus. With associated costs, this comes to $20,250, gives us a total cost structure of $20,460.

Your Canvas

Right, go ahead now and fill in the numbers for your own Canvas. Feel free to use the calculator provided, which can be downloaded using the link I gave you earlier in this chapter.

Value Added: What Value Will Your Employee Add?

In this chapter, which covers the final box of our Lean Recruiting Canvas, we're going to examine our Value Added. In the previous chapter, we looked at the Cost Structure and now it's time to find out if our efforts going forward will be worth it to the company by bringing Cost Structure and Value Added together to determine our Return-on-Investment (ROI).

Let's have a look at what we mean by Value Added. I'm sure you have a good idea in your head of what I'm talking about, but let's start with a solid definition so that we're all on the same page.

By Value Added, I'm talking about value added to a company, normally in monetary terms, by recruiting a new employee.

Profit Center Employees

A Profit Centre Employee is an employee to whom company revenue can be directly attributed. "A profit center is a branch or division of a company that is accounted for on a standalone basis for profit calculation. A profit center is responsible for generating its own results and earnings."[33] Normally, this pertains to the sales and marketing people.

To give you an example of this, let's say in our Cost Structure we worked out that the total cost for hiring a new technical salesperson would be $250,000 a year. Now, that's a fair chunk of change so they'd have to be worth it. If their revenue, however, is anticipated to be a million, then that's a very worthwhile investment.

This certainly doesn't take into account all factors. You have to also consider the other running expenses and daily costs that will also be incurred as during the sales process, such as the cost of support staff, rent and utilities. If you think back to our cost calculations in the previous chapter, this is why we multiplied staff salaries by 1.5 - to take into account all of these other expenses. However, if they're bringing in a million dollars a year, and the role costs you $250,000 plus all of those other expenses, it's safe to say that the hire is probably worthwhile anyway.

And how about marketing people? There was a time not so long ago when it was very challenging to precisely attribute revenue to marketing people. Now, in the age of digital marketing where you can see a lead come through on a website, track it through a UTM code, and follow it all the way through to completion of the sale, it is much easier to accurately attribute some, if not all, of the revenue generated to a marketing person's efforts.

Cost Center Employees

But, it's not just about bringing the money in. It's also about saving money, right? Let's look at Cost Center Employees.

"A cost center is a department within an organization that does not directly add to profit but still costs the organization money to operate. Cost centers only contribute to a company's profitability indirectly, unlike a profit center, which contributes to profitability directly through its actions."[34]

In classic terms, Cost Center Employees are viewed more of as an expense than an investment because their work cannot be directly attributable to a profit center. These are the employees who aren't directly responsible for bringing money in but are necessary for the smooth running of the company. This normally includes employees in accounting, HR, logistics, and even in facilities and maintenance. In most cases, these employees save you money either directly, or indirectly.

An obvious example would be hiring a new accountant who helps you reduce losses through improved efficiencies in the accounting system. If they notice that the company is paying too many taxes, and they've plugged that hole, then they have saved the company money.

Indirect Value Added

More indirectly, by hiring someone, there will be improved morale due to more reasonable workloads. As a result, fewer people will quit, which means your hiring and on-boarding costs will go down. This example is definitely Value Added, but it's really hard to put a number on it because it is three, four or more links down the value chain. But, this is not to say that it isn't valuable at all, right?

---

[34] https://www.investopedia.com/terms/c/cost-center.asp

We're ideally looking for a monetary figure for our Value Added box, even if it is just a 'best guess', but that's not always going to be possible.

Think about public sector employees. The revenue of their employers cannot really change as it comes through taxation, and employees really have no ability to affect that. So our Value Added could be fewer complaints from customers who, of course, are the taxpayers. I would say that's a pretty good value add.

What if you can't think of any Value Added? Does that mean there is none? Not necessarily. What you really need to think about is the cost of doing nothing. Ask yourself, "What bad things will happen if we don't hire someone?" There could be real tangible things with financial costs that could happen. Or, even intangible things.

In contrast, if you and your colleagues, after lots of brainstorming and wringing of hands, truly cannot think of a Value Added for an employee, then maybe there just isn't one. Maybe the hire is superfluous and you don't need to make a hire. Or, maybe you are hiring the wrong person. In any case, finding out that you don't really need to hire someone is a good result because you have determined this before you have gone and sourced someone.

CRAIG E BROWN

Value Added Examples

In each of our examples, we will attempt to determine a financial Value Added. And if we cannot calculate a financial Value Added, then we will attempt to determine a non-financial one. In all our examples we will also try to figure out what the ROI is for each hire.

iOS Developer

Since this developer works for a digital agency, his role falls more into a profit centre category. By contrast, if this developer worked for a company where he was doing internal work on a product for the company, he would more likely be a cost center employee.

For a profit center employee, we should be able to work out how much his efforts are contributing to the bottom line of the company. He is initially being hired to save a contract with a current client but going forward he will be contributing to other projects and adding value elsewhere. Let's say he is on a team of five developers who all work together to fulfill client orders as a unit - one iOS Developer, one Android Developer, one front-end Web Developer, one back-end developer and a DevOps person.

Through their combined efforts, they fulfill $2.3 million worth of orders per year, of which approximately one fifth can be attributed to our iOS Developer - $460,000. That's the number we fill in when completing our Value Added box.

To calculate our Return-On-Investment, simply divide the number in our Value Added box by the number in our Cost Structure box, and multiply by 100 to give a percentage. In this case, 676%, which is a very good return. You will also want to make a note of that figure in the Value Added box.

You could get even more granular and develop your own formula. You will, however, run the risk of overdoing it.

Remember, we are really just trying to show the business that we have done our calculations and that we have given thought to such things. And, of course, we are trying to flag any issues for ourselves.

Inside Sales Representative

Sales professionals are straight-up profit center employees. Let's have a look at our ISR. According to our Canvas, we are losing about $450,000 in missed leads, and we have put him down for an ambitious quota of $500,000. If he hits his target, this will be his Value Added. Simple enough.

To determine the ROI for this role, we simply divide his Value Added by his Cost Structure figure, and again, multiple by 100 to give a percentage. Since his Value Added is $500,000, and his Cost Structure figure is $90,203.33, our ROI is 554%.

Once again, we could get into far more detail when determining Value Added and Cost Structure, but the calculations we have done above will be more than adequate for our purposes.

Administrative Assistant

The situation becomes a bit more complicated for our Administrative Assistant. This person is not a Profit Center employee, and arguably neither is her boss, the CEO.

But, there is always money involved - you just have to dig a little. Let's look at it from this point of view. The reason we need her is because the CEO is getting bogged down in her own administrative tasks, which is not what she has been hired for.

The CEO should be focussed on high-value tasks, such as deciding sales and marketing strategy for example. Let's say for argument's sake that when she spends time on high-value tasks, she is worth to the company $500 per hour. If the new Administrative Assistant can save the CEO 16 hours per week of administrative tasks, this amounts to $8,000 per week in saved costs, or Value Added. This amounts to approximately $360,000 per year ($8,000 per week / 5 days per week × 225 working days per year). That's impressive.

In this case, to calculate ROI, we divide our value add of $360,000 by the Value Added of the Administrative Assistant, which is $13,500, then multiply by 100 for our percentage. Our ROI in this instance is 3,750%. Interestingly, even though this is not a Profit Center employee, she has by far the highest ROI of all our case studies.

Your Canvas

You know what to do. Break out the calculator and fill in your numbers. It might be fairly straightforward as in our first two examples, or you might have to get a little creative as we did in our final example. Remember to calculate your ROI and put that in your Valued Added box as well.

3. PUTTING YOUR PLAN TO THE TEST

Congratulations! You have now completed your Lean Recruiting Canvas. You are a rock star!

It's your second version, but it's really your first full, well thought-out version. So now, I'd like you to step away from the Canvas. You need to go take a break. You've been working hard on it. When you go away and come back, you'll be able to review your work with a fresh set of eyes and have a more objective viewpoint. At this stage, you have been so immersed in the Canvas that objectivity is near impossible. As the English say, 'You can't see the forest for the trees.'

So, go ahead and take that break now. Take at least 45 minutes and then move on to the next section.

Canvas Review

Welcome back! The next step is to review your Canvas before you actually go ahead and do a search. You should do this to ensure you haven't missed anything. Have a look at your Canvas again, and read it like you would a novel. You need to do this so you can read it holistically and objectively, as if a stranger had picked it up and read it for the first time. Don't focus so much on every single point, just read it, skip from part to part, go back and forth and see if anything from a very high level doesn't make sense. Make any corrections that you feel are necessary. Draw it out on a fresh Canvas if you need to. Do that now. Take 5 or 10 minutes.

Read the Canvas like a Novel

I'm going to go to one of my own examples for this section, namely the iOS Developer role. If you would like a copy, you can download it, and the two other completed Canvas examples, at...

http://canvasexamples.JustInTimeRecruiting.com

So here we are, back with my iOS Developer Lean Recruiting Canvas. My first step of course is to go through it and read it, just like I would a book or an article. You can do this with your own completed Canvas as we progress through this chapter. Read it for Lean. By this I mean make sure that it is concise and to the point. Make sure there are no extraneous points. They are wasteful time-killers.

Let's go through the Canvas quickly. We'll start with the Problem. We've been through this before, so we'll just hit each box quickly again because we've just had our break. So our Problem is someone just quit, and the development team is worried that a delay in completing a project will result in bad relations with our client. We worked out that our Solution is indeed to hire someone who is an experienced iOS Developer who can publish, and has published in the past, multiple game apps. We want to make the hire within one month to initially help complete an important client project.

We've said we are the only company that provides integrated iOS apps, Android apps, Web solutions, and even a bit of Internet of Things development in the whole of Ireland. And, that's what is in our Company USPs box.

That looks pretty cool. If a prospective employee sees that they're going to think, "Wow, that's a very kind of niche area and it looks like something I'd be interested in."

You may remember that the role UVP consists of three main parts that come together to form one message.

• Work on exciting project for agency clients in variety of industries – never boring
• Amazing office – pool table, free lunch, dogs
• Flexible working

So, first of all, the person we hire will have cool and challenging work. They'll get to work on an app initially for one client, followed by a variety of other projects. Secondly, the office location has a lot of attractive features. Remember this person is probably going to be fairly young and out of university just a few years. The work environment is going to be quite important to them. Our office is a converted factory in a very cool part of town with an open plan workspace and lots of windows and natural light coming in. On a more practical note, we have a flexible working option. This will serve to both attract and retain this employee.

Under Ideal Employee, here are our bullets for this role...

- Bachelor's Degree in Computer Science or Electrical Engineering
- Great knowledge of Swift programming language
- Object-oriented programming experience
- Multiple published iOS apps

They will have a degree in Computer Science or Electrical Engineering as a bare minimum, as well as great Swift and Object-Oriented programming knowledge. And they must have multiple published iOS apps they can speak to.

We'll go down to Key Metrics and examine what we're going to measure. Here are our bullets from this section...

- Screening call to Coding Test
- Coding Test to Panel Interview
- Panel Interview to Offer
- Offer to Checks
- Checks to Contract

Sources? Our bullet points for this box will look like this...

- Boolean search Indeed / LinkedIn

- Job ad
- Hybrid announcements (social, referrals, hackathon)

We've decided for Sources, we're going to do a Boolean search, and of course publish a killer job advertisement - more about that later. We are then going to take advantage of the passive sources we have set up and send out some announcements via our social media, referral and hackathon channels.

As for Process, here are our steps...

1. Source candidate.
2. Screen for 'Swift', 'Object-oriented' and links to published apps.
3. Screening call to sell opportunity and make them feel the love.
4. Email them with link to coding test. In the same email, outline entire recruiting process from start to finish - it helps them follow along.
5. If they pass coding test, panel interview to verify coding test, assess motivation and general fit with the team.
6. Make an offer.
7. Conduct checks to verify their degree and employment history.
8. Have them sign a contract.

And finally, we examine our Cost Structure and Value Added to determine if we have sufficient ROI to proceed.

OK, now that we have had a quick read, made any necessary corrections, and internalized everything, we will get more granular by doing a Cross-Block Review.

Cross-Block Review

This is a very, very simple process. But it is 100% necessary, so please do not leave it out. All that a Cross-Block Review consists of is looking at each of these boxes individually and comparing the information in the box with the information that's in all of the other boxes, one at a time. You may have picked up on a couple of things already. It should take you no more than 10 minutes once you do it a few times.

Here's how it works. Put your finger, or pen, on one box and compare this information with the information in each of the other boxes, one at a time. That's it. Very simple. You are looking for inconsistent information and checking your work before heading into the Execution Phase.

For example, look at your Problem box and read it, and then you read your Company USPs. Does this information line up? Does it match? Or, are there inconsistencies that need resolving?

Then compare your Problem box to your Role USPs box, and then to your Solution box, and so on. Once you've compared every box on your Canvas with Problem, you then move on to compare the next box with every other box on your Canvas. You continue to do this with each one until they are all completed.

It might be useful at this stage to give you a couple of examples of the kind of information that could be inconsistent and would need to be altered on your Canvas.

For a Software Developer, you may find that you have not included a way to measure technical acumen in your Process. You would therefore need to update your Process accordingly. With a Salesperson, perhaps your panel interview lacks purpose. You would therefore recommend a role-play type panel interview. For an Administrator, you my realize that you are planning to test them on the full suite of Microsoft Office products but they will only really use Word and Outlook in the role, so also testing them on PowerPoint and Excel would be unnecessary and should be removed.

Finish your Cross-Block Review and make adjustments as needed. If your Canvas has become messy, write it out again. Keep track of your versions by writing the version number at the bottom. Remember not to throw out your older Canvases as we're trying to see progression.

Sign-off from Hiring Manager

Now that we're OK with our own Canvas in our own minds, it's time to get our Hiring Manager involved, or the client if you are an agency recruiter. If this is the first time you've interacted with this Hiring Manager about the Process, then you'll probably want to start by sending them an email explaining what the Lean Recruiting Canvas is and does. You can use something like this…

"Hi Sarah,

Thanks for the chat yesterday about the new role. I have put together a plan of action for us using a framework called the Lean Recruiting Canvas. The purpose of it is to make sure that we get the best hire as quickly as possible (without forgetting any factors) by taking a few minutes to plan things out."

Depending on the outcome with the Hiring Manager, you might need a fourth version of your Canvas to incorporate her changes, but that's okay. Keep all your versions and you'll able to learn from them down the road.

What we're really looking for is sign-off from the Hiring Manager. Why is this important? It forces the Hiring Manager to review your assumptions, which should increase their buy-in, particularly if they do have feedback. More importantly, it gives them a last chance to have input.

In order to get sign-off, we'll continue the email above with…

"Have a look at the attached plan. When you have reviewed it, please reply to this email indicating that you have (a) read the plan and (b) agree to it. Once you have replied, I can get started on the search right away."

By using this kind of phrasing, you're letting the Hiring Manager know that nothing will progress until everybody has agreed to the plan. You are also committing the Hiring Manager to replying to you by email, which means they will read the plan, 100% guaranteed. This applies to agency recruiters as well. If they are stuck for an employee, the Hiring Manager will read your Canvas and come back to you quickly. And, if they are not committed, you will not hear back. In this case you may have just saved days, or weeks, of wasted effort.

So, let's say we've competed these steps, emailed the Hiring Manager and she says, "Look, I have a few questions about this, please come and see me." We will then need to drop by her office. Generally speaking, the Hiring Manager is going to be fine with the Problem and the Solution and they may also be fine with the Company USPs and Role UVP. If they have any issues at all, the two areas they're most likely to push back on is the Ideal Employee or the Process.

Regarding the Ideal Employee, it is possible there may be discrepancies between what you have identified as necessary and what the Hiring Manager thinks is required. You'll need to make sure you explain the links between the Ideal Employee, the Problem your company needs solved, and the Solution. There need to be direct links, which is why we have spent so much time checking our work beforehand.

The Hiring Manager may also be too focussed on nice-to-haves. If so, you'll need to explain that you have to focus on must-haves first, and that nice-to-haves can come into play once all of the must-haves have been met by a number of candidates.

The other area the Hiring Manager may be more likely to want to discuss is the Process. A lot of companies have a company-wide processes for interviewing and hiring people, but this is not always appropriate for every role, as we have already gone over.

In fact, it's very rarely appropriate. Your Process should depend on the skill set required for the role. In this instance, you can explain to the Hiring Manager why you chose each step of the Process that you have. She still may not be happy and she might want to do it another way. Everyone has to be on the same page before pushing ahead, so the two of you will have to come to some sort of resolution before you advance to the search.

Resistance

One more quick note about meeting with the Hiring Manager. You may encounter (depending on the individual) some resistance. The Hiring Manager could become annoyed that you are grilling them and asking them to revisit the justification for the hire. After all, they have made the decision they need to hire someone, and they have decided what steps are required to do so. Who are you to question their decision?

If you encounter resistance, try this; it works every time for me. Tell them that starting with the best information possible at the outset will mean that you won't have to come back to them on multiple occasions with follow-up questions. And, that it will help you get them the best candidate faster. I have never had this fail. You are showing them that this process is best for them because, in the long run, their time will not be wasted.

Recap

You'll be happy to know that this ends the planning phase of this book. You might think to yourself that the planning phase has taken quite a bit of time, maybe a few hours. Here's what I would say to you...

Once you have had a bit of experience with this, in the future it should only take you 20 minutes or so to complete a Lean Recruiting Canvas.

If you are hiring for similar roles in the future, very little will likely have to change on the Canvas.

If you plan well, you will waste little time during the Execution phase – and that is, after all, the whole point of this book.

CRAIG E BROWN

Execute the Process

Now it's time to execute the Process you created on your own Lean Recruiting Canvas. At this point, I cannot give you specific guidance on a Process that is unique to your circumstances. Instead, this chapter will focus on giving you tips on common challenges you are likely encounter, and some ideas on making your process as efficient as possible.

Tip 1 - Create a great job ad

Make sure that you craft a well written job advertisement and not just a job description. What's the difference? A job description is used more for internal purposes. It's a list of duties and typically very long. A job description usually includes every single thing that this person is going to do when they get hired. This is not what you want a job advertisement to be.

A job advertisement is a marketing document. And like most marketing documents, if it's well written, it will have one purpose. And that purpose is to get the right 'somebody' to click the 'Apply' button and drop their resume in the hat.

That's all.

Simply put, if your job advertisement is well written, you will have a much greater chance of having the right candidate apply for the job - as opposed to you spending hour after hour conducting searches. If you are conducting searches, a well written advertisement can also mean that when you reach out to a candidate with a link to the ad, they will like what they see and respond to you.

Take the time to write your job advertisement well. I have often encountered job ads that fail to communicate the quality of the role. They are either too short and don't really give the candidate enough information, or they are too long and the relevant information gets buried. So remember, the whole job application process in not only about the candidate trying to sell themselves to you, but also about you selling the role and the company to them. You have to give them something worth applying for.

Let me show you an example of a job advertisement that I found online. We'll see what it looked like both before and after I made changes to it.

Before

Vice-President of Sales

About the role:

We are looking for the next key hire in our leadership team. Specifically, we are in need of an experienced sales leader to take {company name} to the next stage of our journey in creating value for our customers through cutting edge content analysis technologies. This is a growth-focused role with direct responsibility for revenue goals, go-to market strategy, and building and coaching a high output sales team.

Key responsibilities:

- Take full responsibility for revenue growth and the company's sales targets
- Develop and refine scalable sales processes and procedures
- Build an enterprise-focused go-to-market strategy and further grow our cloud business
- Build and manage successful sales teams (inside sales, corporate sales, pre-sales and customer success)
- Develop and implement a partner/channel sales strategy
- Take a hands-on approach to every stage of the sales cycle from prospecting to closing
- Responsibility for key KPIs and metrics (MRR, ARPA, CAC, Churn)
- Identify key market trends and activity that affect the direction of the organization

Skills and experience:

- Experience working in technology and more specifically with data analytics-focused products and teams
- Previous experience bringing a company from $1M ARR to $5M+ ARR (indicative numbers to reflect our stage)
- Previous experience growing and running a high-performing SaaS or Technology sales team
- Proven record managing both transactional and strategic sales cycles
- Track record hiring and coaching a successful sales team
- The ability to build lasting relationships with customers and partners

After

{company name} is the world leader in leveraging Artificial Intelligence to empower thousands of forward-thinking enterprises and developers to collect, analyze, and understand vast amounts of human-generated content.

Every day, we help our users gather and ingest millions of pieces of content to obtain new knowledge and insights about the world, as well as our customers, competitors, and markets.

We are currently looking to hire a Vice-President of Sales to head up our sales operations globally from our new Manhattan office.

This role will allow you to work in a cutting-edge industry at a progressive company that is already cash-flow positive and backed by major investors. This role boasts competitive salary and benefits, and flexible work hours, as well as generous paid vacation allotment.

Responsibilities

- Grow revenue and the company's sales targets
- Build and manage successful sales teams
- Develop key KPIs and metrics

About You

- Significant experience managing data analytics-focused products and teams
- Proven experience growing and running a high-performing SaaS team
- Track record hiring and coaching successful sales teams

Sound interesting? <u>Apply Now</u>!

--

If you have already gone through the earlier sections of this book, particularly the Company USPs, the Role UVP and the Ideal Candidate sections, you should notice a marked difference between these two job ads, even though they are for exactly the same role. The first one is mainly a list of responsibilities, while the second is a marketing document aimed at drawing the candidate in.

In the 'Before' ad, there is no mention of the Company USPs. In fact, there is very little mention of the company at all. What do they do? Who knows? There was a hyperlink back to the company in the online ad, but that required multiple clicks to get to what the company actually does. If you make readers dig for selling points, you will lose them. Put them right on your advertisement as I did in the second version. I actually found this information buried on their website, but the path wasn't obvious.

In the fourth paragraph of the 'After' ad, I state the Role UVP, namely that the role has a competitive salary, benefits, flexible work hours and generous vacation days. As this person, whether male or female, will likely be fairly senior in their career, they will be interested in health benefits, a pension, holidays and getting the kids to soccer practice on time (flexible hours). Also, Manhattan is terrible to commute in, so the odd day working from home would be well appreciated.

I also chopped down the bullet points significantly. In the first ad, many of the bullets reflected things that would be could be assumed for a role this senior. Others are too specific. For the really specific ones, these are the things I would want to check on the phone without giving the game away too early.

And let's not forget the call-to-action at the end. It sounds silly, but it works.

The general flow of the second one is much smoother. The advertisement makes you want to keep reading, because it just keeps getting better and better. The first version is a bit of a chore to read. You find yourself going over the finer points repeatedly to make sure you haven't missed anything. It should be an easier read than that.

Why don't you have a look at some job ads online from random companies? Which ones do you 'get' straight away and which ones require more digging? Which ones contain Company USPs, Role UVP and succinct, but adequately descriptive, responsibility and background bullet points?

Do any of them include a call to action?

It's time to put together your job advertisement now. If you have awkward internal job titles, make sure you use a more generic one so that candidates can actually find your advertisement online. When you are done, show the advertisement to someone who has no involvement whatsoever in your industry and see if they understand it.

Then publish.

Tip 2 - What to cover in the screening call

Firstly, you want to make sure the candidate isn't embellishing the truth about their experience. Before the call, compare their resume with their online profiles for any discrepancies, including dates. Bring these up during the call. If the role calls for the measurement of KPIs and metrics such as MRR, ARPA, CAC and Churn, then ask them what kind types of KPIs and metrics they have experience measuring. Are there any discrepancies in the dates of employment? If so, why? Sometimes candidates just forget to update their online profiles when they lose, or leave, employment.

Secondly, find out the reason the candidate left their last employer or is looking for a new role. If they have left their employer, you may have to read between the lines. In my years of recruitment, I have never met anyone who has admitted to being fired. But of course people do get fired. If they are currently employed, why do they want to leave? Most candidates will be reticent to answer this because they want the call to stay positive. But let's face it, people don't look for a new job if everything is going really well where they are. Try explicitly telling them that you are attempting to draw the real reason out of them by saying something like "Jon, I understand you are trying to be positive about wanting to move a new position as this is an interview, but people don't change jobs if they are happy where they are. What is it about your current role that has prompted you to seek a new position?"

Next, check their attitude. Do they really want this job? Really? Do they sound confident?

Make sure you draw their salary requirements out of them. In most jurisdictions it is perfectly legal to ask someone how much they currently make, but not in all. I usually give them an option. "Jon, can you either tell me how much you are currently making, or what sort of salary you would like to see in this new role?"

And finally, sell the role. Sell, sell, sell. Once you get the information you need from the candidate, tell them all about the company and the role. Spend a good 10 or 15 minutes on it. Much of this will already be on the job ad, but this is your opportunity to go into much greater detail about why this is a fantastic role. If you manage to sell the candidate on the role, they will be (a) more excited by the opportunity, (b) more likely to finish the hiring process, and (c) more willing to forego other opportunities they are looking into.

Tip 3 - Explain the whole hiring process to the candidate

After you get off the phone with the candidate, send them an email outlining the entire recruiting process, and why each step is necessary. This will ensure buy-in from the candidate and increase the chances they will get to the finish line. Here's some standard wording to use for the Inside Sales Representative role.

"Hi Jennifer,

Thanks for the chat a moment ago. As discussed, I have sent your resume across to the Hiring Manager. He should come back to me within one working day with a response.

I'd like to give you a little more information on the rest of the hiring process, so you can follow along and know where you are at any given time.

1. Behavioral assessment - to assess if your behaviors are a fit with this role
2. Panel interview – Remote role play - to check your presentation and persuasion skills, and also your ability to learn new information quickly
3. Make an offer
4. Conduct background checks – income & references - we check income to verify claims of quota achievement
5. Sign contract"

One other positive side-effect of telling candidates about the steps in the process is that it will eliminate a certain amount of embellishment. For example, if a salesperson sees that you will be checking past income as a means of verifying quota achievement, they will likely back out of the process if they have been 'massaging' their numbers. Better now than six months from now when they are in the job.

Tip 4 - Remind Hiring Manager of Process

A bit of time may have passed since you agreed to the Process with the Hiring Manager. When you submit a candidate for review, at least the first time, remind the Hiring Manager of the Process, with an indication of the turnaround times. Put it in terms of candidate expectations. No one likes to keep someone waiting at the door.

You can try something like this...

"Hi Jim,

Happy to say I have our first candidate for the iOS Developer role. I have attached his resume, and my notes on our initial conversation are at the bottom of this email. I have informed the candidate of our process and let him know that you will come back to us within one working day with your thoughts on whether he should progress further.

To refresh your memory, here is the entire recruiting process for this role as we agreed...

1. Sourcing
2. Screening call
3. Coding test
4. Panel interview – check results & fit
5. Make an offer

6. Conduct checks – degree and employers
7. Sign contract

I look forward to your response..."

Phrased this way, it will be clear to Jim that if he delays, he is not just holding you up, but also the applicant. The above approach should help him handle the application with a bit more urgency.

Tip 5 - Reject candidates professionally and quickly

We're all grownups. Candidates hope for the best but are aware that they often won't make it to the final hurdle. If this is the case, don't draw it out. And don't avoid the matter. Break up with them quickly and efficiently. You also want to make sure you don't give candidates ammunition for rebuttal.

Try something like this...

"Hi Jay,

I have heard back from the Hiring Manager and, unfortunately, she is not interested in proceeding further with your application at this stage.

If we have other openings that come up that may be suitable, would it be alright to get back in touch with you?"

You will notice that we have not given the candidate a reason for an unsuccessful application. It may seem unfair, but you must bear in mind that you will be dealing with dozens, if not hundreds, of candidates, most of whom will ultimately be rejected. You simply do not have the time to get into debates with candidates or provide career counselling. This is an unfortunate truth of the digital age. On the flipside, most candidates will be happily surprised that you have come back to them with an email, as many employers today don't bother to reach out due to the volume of candidates they are dealing with.

The final sentence about other roles will keep them on board should other roles come up. It also lessens the blow of rejection and reduces the likelihood of the candidate coming back to you with a rebuttal.

CRAIG E BROWN

Kaizen: Catalyst-Triggered Improvements

The odds of you getting through the entire hiring process without having to make any changes are pretty slim, particularly if it is the first time you have attempted to make a placement for this specific role with this specific employer.

As you will have seen from building your Canvas, there are simply too many moving parts - too many people with conflicting motivations. There are too many ever-shifting environments within your company, your industry and the economy as a whole for there to be a firm likelihood that you get from start to finish with making any alterations.

That's OK.

This is why we have built our Canvas to be Agile. We can change direction at a moment's notice should circumstances dictate. Our strategy will continue to improve over time - this is our Kaizen principle of continuous improvement - until we hit the bullseye and land the right candidate for the job.

So, how do we know when our Lean Recruiting Canvas strategy needs tweaking? We encounter a Catalyst.

A Catalyst is "an agent that provokes or speeds significant change or action."[35] In other words, it is an event or factor that prompts us, or even forces us, to change our Lean Recruiting Canvas.

There are two kinds of Catalysts: Obstructive Catalysts™ and Latent Catalysts™.

Obstructive Catalysts™

An Obstructive Catalyst is an event or other factor that prevents us from moving any further forward with our recruiting efforts. It becomes impossible unless we change our strategy.

You know you have encountered an Obstructive Catalyst when you have come to a dead end in the midst of executing the strategy outlined in your Lean Recruiting Canvas. You do not have to look for this kind of Catalyst. It comes to you. Let's look at a few examples.

The most common example of an Obstructive Catalyst is when you are unable to locate any suitable candidates to put forward. You have searched and searched, but there is no one. Perhaps the role is located in a smaller urban area, or perhaps in remote area, and there is no one with the specialized skill set required to fill the role. Or maybe it is the wrong time of year. It is notoriously difficult to find employees in certain fields in the month of August, and also any time between November 1st and December 31st.

This type of Catalyst can also take another form. Let's say we have advertised for our Administrative Assistant job and we get 125 applicants in a week. Of those, none of them are

---

[35] https://www.merriam-webster.com/dictionary/catalyst

suitable enough to progress to the next step of our Process. None. This is tough because we have agreed on what we're looking for and the Process with the Hiring Manager.

Another common Obstructive Catalyst is if the Hiring Manager informs you that the hire is no longer required. As HR professionals, we normally we don't fight this, but it is worth looking into a bit more.

I am sure there are more. You will recognize the feeling of futility. You know that no matter how much elbow grease you put in, it just isn't going anywhere. But you know you have to do something.

Latent Catalysts™

Latent Catalysts are Catalysts that are not easily recognized without scheduled examination.

An example of a Latent Catalyst might be you noticing that some of the candidates getting through to the final panel interview don't actually match all of the role requirements. This can be for a number of reasons. Maybe the Hiring Manager is in a hurry and thinks 'good enough' is good enough'. Or perhaps the Process is not adequately filtering out unsuitable candidates. A Latent Catalyst is generally a catalyst that might slip through the cracks until after the person is hired. Sometimes they can even develop into Obstructive Catalysts during the hiring process itself. Wouldn't it be nice if there was a way to head them off before it got that serious?

There is.

Block off a slot on your calendar every week. As little as 30 minutes should do the trick, depending on how many roles you are working on. I normally go with Friday at 2pm. For me, this is a good time because my brain is a bit burnt out from focusing during the rest of the work week.

This time allows me to see things a bit more holistically and objectively. Some people prefer Monday morning after they come back from the weekend refreshed. It's up to you, but make sure you put it in your calendar. It is really important. If that slot in your calendar gets taken over by something else, perhaps a mandated meeting, take a minute to move your Canvas review to another slot. If you don't, then another week will pass before you realize you have hit a snag. This snag can then potentially escalate to an Obstructive Catalyst.

During this time you have assigned, you should pull out your Canvases and ask yourself how things are going. It's pretty simple. Are you getting in enough candidates in the pipeline who are meeting the Ideal Candidate criteria? If not, why not? Are your ratios low enough between steps in your Key Metrics box? Are your candidates being kicked back at the panel interview stage? Why? Are you losing candidates to competing employers? Why?

Go through the Canvas, box by box - hold your finger or pen down on each box so you don't lose your place - and compare that with reality. If reality is not living up to the strategy, then something has to change.

CRAIG E BROWN

250

4. Agile – Changing Directions

So, you have hit a snag. You have encountered a Catalyst. Whether it's an Obstructive Catalyst or a Latent Catalyst, what to do next is one of the main points of this book.

If you encounter a Catalyst, do something about it. Do it quickly and decisively.

Remember, hope is not a strategy. The issue will not go away on its own.

Here are the basic steps you will need to work through in order to overcome a Catalyst.

Step 1. Identify the Catalyst

Step 2. Alter the Lean Recruiting Canvas to compensate

Step 3. Get buy-in

Step 4. Execute

Let's go back to our three example Canvases and add in three common Catalysts. If you haven't already, you can download the completed Canvases at...

http://examplecanvases.JustInTimeRecruiting.com.

iOS Developer

In this case, we have found that we have encountered an Obstructive Catalyst. We simply have not been able to find any suitably qualified iOS Developers in our local area. It happens.

The person we are looking for needs to be fairly talented and experienced, and we live in a smaller city, like Limerick in the west of Ireland. We have searched and searched and searched, and have not found a single qualified, adequately experienced developer who can help us.

Now that we have identified our Catalyst, we have to think of a few alternative courses of action. The first option we can consider is to hire a remote worker. This may not be everyone's first choice, particularly if the employer hasn't hired remote workers before. However, if a candidate's experience is at the level that we need, their level of English is also good, and they have experience working remotely, then there's no reason why we shouldn't consider this option.

We also may wish to consider relocating candidates from other parts of the same country or from another country altogether. Since we're in Ireland, we are fortunate because in the European Union, any citizen of any one of the more than two dozen member countries is legally permitted to move to, and work in, any other European Union country without a visa. As a result, we could try to find iOS Developers of suitable quality in Spain, Romania or Italy, and then relocate them to Ireland for the role.

If you live in another part of the world such as Canada or the United States, you could also consider helping candidates move from other countries, but your company would need to have significant immigration assistance experience. It would probably be easier to just move someone from a different part of your own country.

Another option is just to wait. Over time, you can keep promoting the position via your social media and referral channels. You can also continue to publish the job advertisement online, and perhaps, things will pick up. This could very well be a viable option if you're not in any particular hurry to hire the candidate. But it's probably not a great option for us because we have time constraints associated with this hire.

Whichever option, or options, you choose, the next step will be to go back and alter your Lean Recruiting Canvas.

Step three is securing buy-in on the change. You need to go back to the Hiring Manager and illustrate to them not only the problem you're having, but all of the steps that you've taken to find a suitable candidate. Illustrating all of the steps you have taken to date will align the Hiring Manager with your thought process and actions.

Inside Sales Representative

This time, for the Inside Sales Representative role, you have encountered a Latent Catalyst. Friday afternoon has come around, and you have set time aside to go over all of your Canvases, and you notice something interesting. Your panel interview-to-offer ratio has ballooned recently. In fact, no one is getting past the panel interview at all, so you start investigating the cause.

You speak to two of the four panel members who have conducted the interview. They inform you that they have been disappointed by the fact that none of the candidates you have put forward have any formal sales training experience such as Sandler Training. The candidates have lots of practical experience and proven track records, but really, one of the things they're looking for is formal sales training experience.

Unfortunately for you, this is the first time you've heard about this requirement. At no stage during the strategy creation and execution did anyone indicate that formal sales training was a requirement. It would have been ideal to have learned about this three weeks ago, but it's better to find out now than in another three weeks. That's the value of performing weekly checks for Latent Catalysts. We can find little problems before they become big problems.

Now that you have identified this Catalyst, we will add the extra requirement to the Ideal Candidate box, change our job advertisement and re-publish it. Finally, we will make a note to bring this point up when we are conducting our initial screening reviews with job candidates. Then, we execute our strategy once again.

Administrative Assistant

For our final position of Administrative Assistant, we have encountered an issue. It's more of a Latent Catalyst. We didn't notice it in our weekly review, but it has slowed things down to a crawl and become noticeable on its own.

We are getting lots of candidates applying, and a sufficient number of them are remembering to include the word 'Elephant' in the subject line of their application, showing that they pay attention to detail. We are then conducting screening interviews and many of these candidates are good enough to be moved on to the next stage and be invited in for testing and a panel interview.

The problem is that very few people are passing the typing test. We've indicated that our candidates need to be able to type at 50 words per minute error-free. But if you think about it, do you actually know anyone today who can type at 50 words per minute error-free? Error-free typing used to be a necessity in the days of typewriters when making a mistake meant pulling the paper out, deleting the mistake using liquid paper, waiting for it to dry, and starting over again. Now, of course, when you make a mistake, you see the red squiggly line, and you can go back and correct quickly. I personally can only type about 30 words per minute, and it certainly isn't error-free.

You speak to the Hiring Manager, who in this case is the CEO of the company, and you ask her if the '50 words per minute' stipulation is actually necessary. Many of the candidates are doing 30 words per minute error-free, and some of those candidates have been doing 50 words per minute, but with errors. You also explain the point about misspellings being flagged up automatically. The CEO agrees that the standard can be lowered to 30 words per minute error-free. Now that you have that agreement in place, you just need to adjust the Ideal Candidate profile on your Lean Recruiting Canvas, re-publish the job description, and wait for new candidates to come in.

You can also go back over some of the old candidates who failed the initial typing test, see who passed the new requirements, and get them to come in for full panel interviews.

Your Canvas

If you encounter the need to make changes, which you likely will, particularly for roles you have never filled before for this employer, you will need to update your Canvas accordingly.

Each time you need to make updates, get out a clean Canvas and fill it out. It will only take a couple minutes. The exercise of quickly writing or typing it out again will force you reflect. In addition, doing so will ensure you have a new clear plan of action, and also so that you can see your own progression.

The next time you have to fill this same role, you can go back through your three or four versions of the Canvas, see the progression, what went right and what went wrong. It will help you when interviewing Hiring Managers again for the same role, six months or a year from now.

Persuading the Hiring Manager

At this stage, you may be thinking to yourself, "I have encountered a Catalyst and have identified possible resolutions. How will I convince the Hiring Manager to get on board with the change?"

It is a fair point. Put yourself back in the Hiring Manager's shoes. First of all, they may still be of the mindset that recruiting is actually very easy. They may think that all you do is post the job, collect applicants and put them forward. You have to show them that there is more to it. You can do this by presenting your work to date.

Here are the steps you can take.

Step 1: Present the Catalyst

Step 2: Show the Hiring Manager your initial Canvas(es) again

Step 3: Present your resolution

Step 4: Get sign off

Step 5: Get cracking on implementation

You can see the value in hanging onto your Canvases from the steps above. They help you build a story. They also demonstrate how hard you have been working on this role, and how much thought has gone into it.

So first, you present the Catalyst to the Hiring Manager. It may be a good idea to use a word other than 'Catalyst' when presenting. The Hiring Manager likely won't know what it means in our context here. Perhaps tell them that you have hit a snag. If it is an Obstructive Catalyst, it will be easy to explain. If it is a Latent Catalyst, it will likely require more in-depth explanation as the Hiring Manager may not have realized there is a problem. Explain to them that you noticed it as part of a weekly review process you employ to find trouble spots.

Then, you bring out the initial Canvas that the Hiring Manager signed off on and run through it again with them. At this stage, it should start to become clear to them why the plan needs to change. If you are looking for an iOS Developer with 5 years' experience, and there are only iOS Developers with 2 years' experience, something has to give.

Then present the Hiring Manager with your possible solutions. If you are presenting a problem, you should always present at least one solution at the same time. You can even ask them if they have any ideas of their own. This can work well if you have a solid relationship with them.

Between the two of you, you agree on a course of action. Once you have agreement, revise your Canvas and send the Hiring Manager the revised version by email for their records.

Then get cracking on executing the revised Canvas. That's it.

If the Catalyst is that the Hiring Manager has cancelled the requisition, you will have to take a slightly different approach. Although you might be grateful that the requisition has been taken off your desk, you should get to the bottom of why this has been cancelled. If the Problem no longer exists, then fair enough. But it's unlikely.

Assuming the Problem does still exist, you need to find out why the requisition has been cancelled. Remember, if the Problem still exists, then it needs to be rectified. There always needs to be a Solution, even if it isn't to hire someone. The other possibility is that the Problem has morphed into something else. If so, you need to examine the situation and determine if the Solution to the Problem is to hire a different type of person. If this is the case, you need to revise the entire Canvas, get sign off on the Canvas and the requisition and get started again.

.

5. Post Placement Review – Perfecting the Plan

Ideally after no more than one or two adjustments to your Canvas, you have made a successful placement. As one final step to our entire strategy, it is now time to make sure we got it right by doing a post-placement review. This should be performed at three separate stages.

Immediately after the placement is made

Immediately following the placement of a new hire, you should go back over your final Canvas to make sure everything stacked up in the end. Did the person you hire have all of the characteristics and experiences you wanted as listed in the Ideal Employee section? Were your ratios sufficiently low? If not, why? What can you do about this next time?

Go through the entire Canvas and double-check that everything is as it should be. Make notes on the back (or on a clean Canvas, perhaps stapled to this one) giving yourself some tips for the next similar hire. You won't remember all the details later, so writing them down while things are fresh in your mind is imperative.

Annually during the performance review

Also, put a copy of your final Canvas (with notes from above) into the employee's file. You should look at it again when their first, and subsequent, annual performance reviews are conducted. You can check the whole Canvas again, but the emphasis of this review should be on Value Added and Cost Structure, and therefore also ROI.

Really what you are asking yourself here is "Was it worth it to hire this person?"

To give an example, our Inside Sales Representative only sold $420,000 of product, but he was given a quota of $500,000. You investigate and find that there was a three-month ramp-up period before his sales efforts gained momentum. Rather than a total Cost Structure of around $90,000, he only incurred costs of around $80,000. The reduced compensation has resulted from reduced sales thereby affecting the employee's commissions. If you run the calculations, the ROI is still basically the same. There shouldn't really be much cause for concern here so long as his sales are now on consistently on target.

You should also do a quick check over the rest of the Canvas as well. For example, you may have found that your Panel Interview to Offer ratio was fairly high. Our employee has worked out nicely, so perhaps this high ratio is just a result of being very picky. The takeaway here is to find an answer.

Make any further notes you need on your Canvas.

When you need to make a similar hire down the road

This is where everything ties together. The next time you need to hire an Inside Sales Representative (or an iOS

Developer or Administrative Assistant or any other position), your strategy will basically be already written for you. At that stage, you will simply need to review the Canvas again to make sure no external factors have changed, and then push ahead with your strategy. You will likely find that one or two factors have changed, but the vast remainder has stayed constant.

6. Tying It All Together

Since Lean is all about simplicity and cutting out waste, this final chapter summarizes key learning points from each of the salient chapters in this book - one key takeaway for each.

What is Lean Recruiting?

Lean Recruiting is a systematic method for waste minimization within the recruiting process while at the same time increasing productivity. When people think of Lean they normally think about saving money. This is accurate, but it's more about saving time and getting to the ideal hire as quickly and efficiently as a possible.

The Lean Recruiting Canvas

The Lean Recruiting Canvas is a one-page strategy document that allows you to plan, execute and continuously improve your hiring for one specific type of role. The next ten points are boxes in this Canvas.

Problem

The Problem is a clear statement of the business challenge that has led to the role requirement. This should not be confused with the recruiter's problem of being tasked with finding qualified candidates. We need to identify the Problem the company is encountering that made the Hiring Manager decide to hire someone. The best way to discover the Problem is to ask yourself this question: "What bad things will happen to the company if this position is not filled?"

Solution

The Solution is what will make the Problem go away permanently, or semi-permanently for a year, two years or longer. Remember, hiring someone is not the only possible Solution. Other possibilities include hiring a contractor, outsourcing or even doing nothing at all.

Ideal Employee

The three to five bullet points in the Ideal Employee box should be experiences or traits the candidate absolutely must possess to be considered for the position. The word 'must' is critical here. Unless the candidate has every one of these traits / experiences you do not want to speak with them under any circumstances. It takes discipline but is worth the effort.

These can be hard points or soft points but they always must be 'Must-Haves', as opposed to 'Nice-to-Haves', even if it is challenging to prove.

Company USPs

A company's Unique Selling Points (USPs) are product features that makes the company different from, and ideally better than, all its competitors. Quite simply, we want to define what makes the company different from its competitors in the eyes of your customers. If you have both customers and competitors, then there has to be something unique about your company or else your customers wouldn't be buying from you. We evaluate Company USPs to give potential candidates proof that the company is an ongoing, viable concern that will be a stable place to work going forward.

Role UVP

The role's Unique Value Proposition (UVP) is a combination of factors that may not be unique in themselves but when brought together make for a unique, and ideally, irresistible offering for the job candidate. These are the selling points for the role itself. For more mature applicants, it could be things like life insurance, medical and dental coverage, and pension contributions. For more junior candidates, depending on the industry, it could be things like having a games room, free lunches and team outings.

Sources

Sources are the routes through which candidates are found. In keeping with our Lean principles, we are looking to find the best results we can for the least amount of effort. Sources should line up with the type of role and whether or not candidates need to be headhunted or if you expect the job advertisement to draw large numbers. Sources are also influenced by the Ideal Employee profile.

Process

The Process is the series of steps we need to take to hire a new employee. It must be kept as short as possible so that we don't lose a candidate to a rival employer while at the same time proving all of the points in the Ideal Employee box. Remember, the Process is always role-specific. Company-wide recruitment processes don't work.

Key Metrics

Key Metrics are factors that you measure to make sure that your Process and other assumptions are robust. This is where we start laying the foundation for the *Kaizen* theory of continuous improvement. We do this largely by analyzing ratios such as submission-to-screening interview, and panel interview-to-offer.

Cost Structure

The Cost Structure is the annualized cost of recruiting and employing a new employee. Here we are tying hiring requirements back to the requirements of the company to demonstrate value for money to the Hiring Manager.

Value Added

The Value Added is value the new employee brings to the company. Normally expressed in in monetary terms, Value Added quantifies the revenue the role will either bring the company, or save the company from incurring. Calculating Return-on-Investment is key here, which is done by subtracting Cost Structure from our total Value Added.

Putting Your Plan to The Test

This section is all about making the process happen. We have created our plan and it's time to put it to the test. Before starting, take a break to regain objectivity, ideally at least 45 minutes, then push ahead.

Canvas Review

During the Canvass Review, you will read the Canvas like novel and then do a Cross-Block Review to identify any inconsistencies or final points for improvement. The review wraps up with securing sign-off from the Hiring Manager.

Execute the Process

Now it's time to get to work and test what you have created. This section provides helpful tips and advice on some of the more important steps. Detailed insights are given on creating a solid job ad, what to cover in the screening call and informing the candidate of the entire Process. It's also time to bring the Hiring Manager back into the fold by reminding them of the process and reconfirming their buy-in. How to reject unsuccessful candidates professionally and quickly is also covered.

Kaizen: Catalyst-Triggered Improvements

A Catalyst is an agent that provokes or speeds up significant change or action. In other words, it is an event or factor that prompts us, and sometimes even forces us, to alter our Lean Recruiting Canvas.

Obstructive Catalysts™

An Obstructive Catalyst is an event or other factor that prevents us from moving any further with our recruiting efforts. With this kind of catalyst, you will not be able to proceed any further unless you change your strategy.

Latent Catalysts™

Latent Catalysts are Catalysts that are not easily recognized without regular examination. Scheduling Canvas reviews once a week will help ensure you will be able to detect any Latent Catalysts before they become Obstructive Catalysts.

Agile: Changing Directions

If you encounter a Catalyst, the most important thing is to do something about it. Do it quickly and decisively. Remember, hope is not a strategy.

Post-Placement Review

There are three times when you need to review your Lean Recruiting Canvas after the candidate is hired; immediately after the person is hired, during the employee's annual performance reviews, and just before the next similar hire is made.

Final Thoughts

I would like to leave you with one final thought. The Lean Recruiting Canvas and associated strategy is about change. And change is hard. But it is necessary.

"The world as we have created it is a process of our thinking. It cannot be changed without changing our thinking." ~ Albert Einstein

Appendix 1 - Variations

In this book, we've followed the process of putting together a Lean Recruiting Canvas using the route I normally follow, but that doesn't mean you have to do it that way.

The Lean Recruiting Canvas is not a list of bullet points that are executed from start to finish steps one through ten. Instead, you fill in the sections you know and work out the rest.

Using different routes through the Canvas

Let's examine some different routes that you can take through the Canvas, depending on your company's challenges.

Revised Value Added

Our first example is a sales hire, so we'll define our Problem as needing to increase revenue by $1M per year to meet the projections promised to the board. This means our Value Added needs to be $1M or more, depending on the Cost

Structure. Based on the past examples in this book, you may initially think that our Solution is to hire an Inside Sales Representative. The challenge with this is that Inside Sales Representatives at this company usually only bring in about $500,000 per year, which falls short of the $1M Value Added per year that we need. Our Solution, therefore, can't be to hire an Inside Sales Representative. We will instead need to hire a senior-level Software Sales Executive. Software Sales Executives are typically tasked with bringing in between $1M and $2M per year and are normally responsible for generating their own leads.

Now that we have our Solution worked out, we can come back to the Cost Structure and work that out. We'll probably spend about $200,000 per year on this hire (a base salary of $100,000, plus a $100,000 bonus if the sales quota is achieved). From there we can fill in the rest of the Lean Recruiting Canvas based on what we need to do for this role.

Incidentally, quota should be set for about $1.2M or $1.3M to allow for the cost of employing this person.

Company Ambivalent Employees

In this example, we'll investigate a scenario whereby we expect candidates will not really care what company they work for, because they view their role as being fairly junior and more or less generic. Those who are newer to the workforce will not be overly concerned about the company's stability or its reputation. It will be the role itself that will interest them. It's possible that either our Administrative Assistant role, or even our IOS Developer role could fit this description.

One way to approach this scenario would be to first work on the Problem and the Solution, and then move on to the role's

Unique Value Proposition to see if there will be an adequate incentive for the right person to apply for and accept the job. This is particularly important in an economy that is recovering and booming, when candidates typically have the greatest level of choice. In this case, the role will need to be adequately enticing to attract candidates who just want to know what's in it for them.

Using the Canvas for Reasons Other Than Hiring

The Canvas can also be used to help you with non-recruiting HR challenges, depending on the situation. Again, it is up to you where you start, but I will provide you with some examples.

Departmental Closure - Reducing Layoffs

Our next example considers what to do when you have a departmental closure and a series of impending layoffs. A good example may be a company that has experimented with digital inbound marketing, but it hasn't worked out. They decide to scrap the entire inbound marketing department and increase the sales team as a way of making up the revenue. The issue here is that the company now has a group of really good employees who have proven themselves to be diligent, but whose talents will be wasted if they are let go. Letting them go will also incur expenses like severance packages and having to find, and onboard, new employees for the Sales Department.

A Canvas can help us with this scenario. We can start by filling in the Ideal Candidate box. In this example, we have an employee called Cindy who has been working in the Inbound Marketing Department. We go back through Cindy's annual performance reviews and notice some interesting comments about her. Firstly, it's obvious from her reviews that she's a very hard worker. Secondly, she is also very much a strong team player. And thirdly, she is very process-oriented. Cindy's strengths are actually some of the top traits that we would expect to see in a very successful sales person. We write these down in our Ideal Candidate box.

We can then also fill out the Problem box. The Problem here is that the company needs to increase revenues, but the inbound marketing approach hasn't worked out. The Solution is to expand the sales team. We next fill in the rest of the boxes. The Cost Structure box will be very telling in this example, because the numbers will show that retraining Cindy to do sales would be more cost-effective than incurring the costs of laying her off and hiring and onboarding a new employee.

Cost Structure Too High

Here's a final example of a different route you could take through the Canvas. In this scenario, the Cost Structure is too high to hire IOS Developers. Our boss tells us that we need to bring the costs down for any future hires while at the same time maintaining the same level of Value Added. The Problem remains the same as it would for any other IOS Developer hire. Our Solution, however, will need to change.

We propose to the Hiring Manager to hire IOS Developers with between one- and two-years working experience who have solid, proven portfolios online rather than hiring IOS Developers with three to five years' experience. This should get the salaries down by $10,000 to $15,000 per hire, while at the same time maintaining quality. Who knows, maybe we'll even increase the level of quality. We, of course, also need to alter the rest of the Canvas accordingly. We'll need to examine the Company USPs again, the Role UVP, Ideal Employee, Process, Sources and also Key Metrics.

Appendix 2 – Further Information

If you would like further information on how Lean Recruiting methodology can benefit your organization, I am happy to provide a free consultation to go over your requirements – no strings attached.

Simply fill out the following form and I will be in touch: http://Consultation.JustInTimeRecruiting.com

Our services include…

- JIT Recruiting Yellow, Green & Black belt certifications
- eLearning Solutions
- In-Person Training & Mentoring
- Speaking Engagements
- And much more…

You are also very welcome to connect with me on LinkedIn.

Craig
https://www.linkedin.com/in/cebrownmba

ABOUT THE AUTHOR

Craig E. Brown is the author of The Lean Recruiting Toolkit and the founder of JustInTimeRecruiting.com, where his mission is to help companies across the globe find the best talent they can, in the shortest time possible, who will stay with their employers longer.

With a lifelong passion for process optimization, Craig is the creator of the Lean Recruiting Canvas, a one-page strategic framework that is revolutionizing talent acquisition.

Craig regularly trains, mentors and consults with companies around the globe on how to perfect their recruiting processes. He also has almost two decades of experience successfully placing candidates across the English-speaking world and Asia. Roles span from software developers, salespeople, engineers, marketing, HR, finance, educational and operational staff.

Craig has an MBA from Kingston University in England, and a degree in Literature from Acadia University in Canada. He currently resides in Ireland with his wife and three children.

32107419R00163

Printed in Poland
by Amazon Fulfillment
Poland Sp. z o.o., Wrocław